Surrendered

40 Devotions to Help You Let Go & Live Like Jesus

Barb Roose

Abingdon Press | Nashville

Surrendered

40 Devotions to Help You Let Go and Live Like Jesus

Library of Congress Control Number: 2020940202

ISBN 13: 978-1-7910-0799-7

20 21 22 23 24 25 26 27 28 29—10 9 8 7 6 5 4 3 2 1
MANUFACTURED IN THE UNITED STATES OF AMERICA

You can let go.

It will be OK.

God is with you every step of the way.

Mark & Jen—
You are
deeply
loved!
♡ Dana
10/2020

Contents

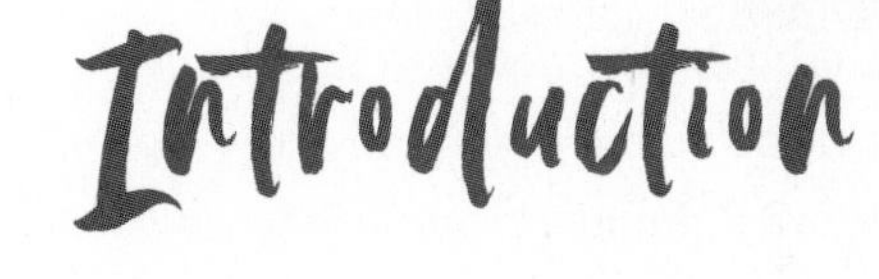

Introduction

Dear friend,

I'm so glad to meet you here as you begin this forty-day journey to let go and live like Jesus, especially if you're in the midst of a hard or heartbreaking season of life. But even if your life feels pretty wonderful right now, you'll still find the journey to be worthwhile as you learn to surrender more and more of your life to Him.

Within these pages, you're invited to embrace the life-giving, life-transforming power of surrender, which is the decision to let go and fully trust God's power, presence, promises, and provision for your life. As you'll discover along the way, surrender is your only path to lasting peace in the midst of painful problems or difficult people. Surrender isn't giving up or giving in; rather, it's the decision to give over whatever you can't control, essentially declaring, *"God, if it's gonna get done, You're gonna to have to do it!"*

What have you been trying to control lately? Do you feel that externally you're doing all you can to keep everything and everyone together, but internally you're about to fall apart? If that's the case, then I want to encourage you to begin this forty-day journey *today*.

When something or someone in your life feels out of control, it's easy to think you've got to fix things on your own or wonder if God has forgotten about you. But that's not true! Before you read any further, I want you to know this: *You are fully seen and completely loved by God, and there is hope for whatever problem or situation you're facing.*

For many years, I tried to fix an addiction problem of a family member. I bargained, begged, and blew up in ugly outbursts of anger because I was frustrated over what I couldn't control. Most of all, I feared what would happen if I failed.

However, as I studied Jesus' time of temptation and trial in the wilderness, I realized that His example of peace and perseverance did not result from trying to force His way. Rather, Jesus relied upon His relationship with the Father to sustain and empower Him in the midst of that difficult situation.

As I learned from Jesus' experience in the wilderness, as well as His life detailed in the Gospels, I discovered more and more how to pray like Jesus, forgive like Jesus, love like Jesus, and most important, surrender like Jesus. The more I applied Jesus' teachings, the more I was able to surrender control to God. This journey toward surrender ultimately delivered me to one of the greatest gifts of all: hope.

Are you looking for hope today? The key is letting go of what you can't control and fully trusting God. That is what it means to surrender. Rather than living stressed out during the day and sleepless at night, it *is* possible to learn to surrender and experience lasting peace.

My prayer is that these devotions will be like a quick cup of "spiritual coffee" for you—a pick-me-up for your soul. Read one devotion each day throughout the forty-day journey, or if you prefer, you can scan the table of contents and pick the topic that most resonates with you. Whether you choose to read at the start of your day to set your mind on God, in the midst of your day to refocus your thoughts (especially when things aren't going your way), or at the end of your day to prepare you for tomorrow, each brief devotion will center you in God's power, presence, promises, or provision. It is my hope that as you reflect on what you've read, the words will perk you up with a jolt of hope or help or a practical next step that you can apply in your life. Each day ends with one of six Surrender Principles, which I expound upon in my six-week Bible study *Surrendered: Letting Go and Living Like Jesus*:

1. I am not in control of others or outcomes.
2. I choose to live by faith, not rush to follow my feelings.
3. I can always let go and give my problems to God.
4. Trusting God's promises will bless me, but pushing my plans will stress me.

5. When fear tempts me to flee, fix, or force my way, I will choose to stop and pray.
6. Surrender is my only path to God's peace, power, and provision.

If you would like to learn more about these principles and equip yourself with more practical tools for the ongoing surrender journey, I encourage you to consider doing the study—whether alone or with a group of friends.

Finally, as you get started, be sure to give yourself grace to grow at your own pace. Learning to let go and live like Jesus isn't a switch that you flip but a process that takes time. My prayer is that you will discover freedom, peace, and hope as you surrender and trust God with your life.

Barb

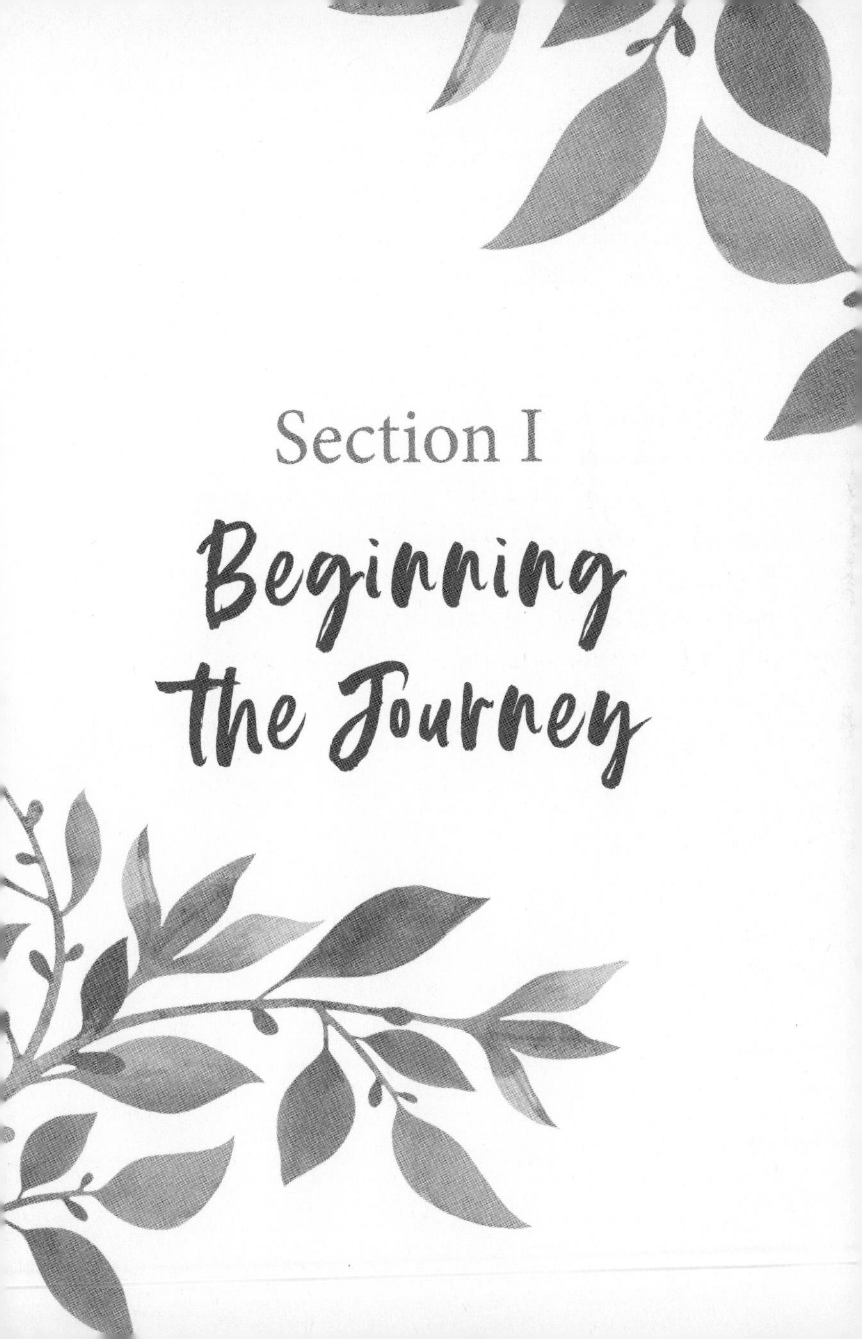

Section I

Beginning the Journey

DAY 1

Waking Up in the Wilderness

The LORD is close to the brokenhearted
and saves those who are crushed in spirit.
(Psalm 34:18)

Have you ever gone to bed feeling like you were on top of the world, and then you woke up one day, and suddenly the world was on top of you?

It's too much, God. I can't handle anything else.

If this is you, here's what I want you to know right now, in this moment:

Dear sister with the weary soul,
you are not alone in your struggle.

God knows the weight you carry.
He hears the cry of your heart. You are seen.
Most of all, you are dearly loved.

Take a moment and let that settle over you.

God is close to you right now. You are not alone. God is present with you. Even more, He is the God who saves. This means that whatever overwhelming situation you're facing, you aren't responsible for fixing it.

We all experience hard and heartbreaking circumstances. At times, those trials spread into long stretches of hardship. Spiritually speaking, we call these periods of time wilderness seasons. These seem to press the pause button in our lives. They are often high-stakes situations with no quick fixes, and we have little to no control over them. Wilderness seasons can feel scary and uncertain. Often, spiritual confusion mounts as we wonder why this is happening, where God is, or what God is doing while our lives feel like they are falling apart around our feet.

During earlier wilderness seasons, I'd scribble the phrase, "God, give me my old life back!" over and over again in my journals. I was afraid, and I felt stuck. I spent years trying to fix and force my way out of problems, only to make things worse. I kept trying to save people and rescue myself. I failed. And my fears overwhelmed me.

The change came when I realized that God loved me too much to give me back the old life I thought I controlled. Rather, He wanted to lead me in another direction: toward His best for me.

To make that journey through the long and difficult wilderness, I had to anchor myself to three truths about God. Here's what I call the Wilderness ABCs:[1]

1. You are **A**lways loved. (Psalm 52:8; Jeremiah 31:3; 1 John 4:19)
2. **B**elieve that God is for you. (Joshua 1:9; Matthew 6:33)
3. **C**hallenge yourself to trust God and let go. (Philippians 1:19)

Whatever you're facing right now isn't the measure of God's love for you.

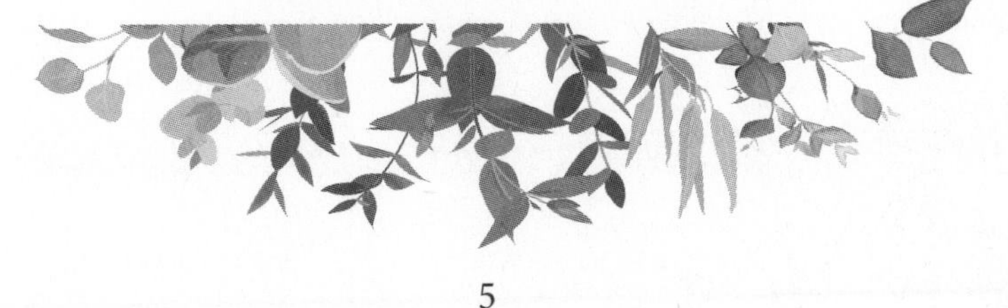

Whatever you're facing right now isn't the measure of God's love for you. His love is and always will be measured by the fact that He sent Jesus to die for you. Don't let your circumstances mislead you into believing that God is out to get you. In fact, God is out to *give* you His best. When you know God always loves you and is for you, you can challenge yourself to trust God.

While you may believe your problems or pain are too much today, know that God loves and cares for you much, much more.

PRAYER: Dear God, in this moment, I know that You are close to me. I am weary and tired from so much. Help me remember that Your love is much greater than whatever pain or problems I'm facing today. Remind me that You are for me, so I can let go of my struggles and trust in You. Amen.

Surrender Principle

Surrender is my only path to peace.

1. Barb Roose, *Surrendered: Letting Go & Living Like Jesus* (Nashville: Abingdon Press, 2020), 47.

DAY 2

Who Is in Control of You?

Letting the Spirit control your mind leads to life and peace. (Romans 8:6b NLT)

Are you a self-described control freak?

I hear this from women all the time: "Oh, I try to control everything." I've never run into a woman who's excited about being a control freak, but many embrace the label anyway. The irony is you try to control others or outcomes, which isn't healthy or helpful, but you don't feel like you can control yourself.

I'm not a fan of the label "control freak" because I believe we're more than our flaws or our struggles. Instead, I prefer the term "control-loving." Control issues are unhealthy behaviors, not your identity. You are God's precious, beautiful, loveable daughter. That is your identity. As you let God transform your

heart, He can transform your control-loving behaviors into attitudes and actions that reflect the beautiful character of Christ.

Where did our struggle with control begin? It's a problem stemming from the days in the garden of Eden—when Adam and Eve ate the forbidden fruit (see Genesis 3). As their descendants, we want what we want when we want it. So, from that self-centered desire springs forth five control-loving behaviors that I describe in my Bible study, *Surrendered: Letting Go & Living Like Jesus*. I developed the acronym SHINE to describe those behaviors:[2]

Stonewalling — shutting down or running away from the problem

Helicoptering —	micromanaging everyone or everything
Interrupting —	stopping someone's words or shutting down their actions
Nagging —	repeated and unsolicited reminders or excessive warnings
Excessive — Stockpiling	Collecting more than what's needed out of fear

Which one or more of these resonates with you?

We use our control-loving behaviors like buttons on a giant remote control. Which SHINE buttons have you been pressing lately? While you might succeed some of the time, that success always comes with a lot of stress.

Just because we might be able to force our solutions on people or our problems, our controlling behaviors never deliver what we truly want: peace. Instead, we become frustrated because we are trying to hold everyone and everything together, and we are terrified of what will happen if it all falls apart.

Perhaps that's why you're reading this devotional.

Here's a painful reality you've likely discovered: **Whatever you're using to control others will eventually begin to control you.**

However, when you let God take control of you, He promises life and peace even in the midst of whatever you're facing right now. God's peace is better than anything you could ever imagine (Philippians 4:7), and God's power can accomplish infinitely more than any control-loving buttons that you could ever push (Ephesians 3:20).

Ultimately, you decide who's in control of you. Do you want to keep trying to fix others and outcomes, or do you want to experience God's life and peace? In the words of a wise man named Moses who spoke for God long ago: choose life (Deuteronomy 30:19).

- Which control-loving behavior(s) can you relate to most?
- What difference could God's peace make in your difficult situation right now?

PRAYER: God, I'm tired of trying to control everyone and everything. I'm ready to let go because I need Your life and peace. Amen.

Surrender Principle

I can always let go and give my problems to God.

1. Barb Roose, *Surrendered: Letting Go & Living Like Jesus* (Nashville: Abingdon Press, 2020), 37.

DAY 3

Three Questions to Start Your Journey

We know that suffering produces perseverance; perseverance, character; and character, hope.
(Romans 5:3b-4)

Many years ago, I reluctantly attended my first family member addiction recovery support group. I'd spent years trying to fix an addiction issue in my family, even forcing solutions when necessary. Nothing worked. In fact, things were getting worse. I was scared, angry, and embarrassed. Walking into that recovery group meeting felt like an admission of failure.

Yet, what felt like a failure was exactly what God used to transform my faith, ultimately giving me what Romans 5:3-4 promises: the strength to endure, Christlike character, and most of all, unshakeable hope.

The start of my journey began with a choice: let go and live by faith or go back to trying to force solutions.

> Letting go isn't as easy as it sounds, is it?
>
> Letting go means there are no guarantees.
>
> Letting go means you have to admit you aren't in control and stop trying to act like God in others' lives.
>
> Letting go means you have to give loved ones the right to make their own decisions, even if those decisions are unhealthy.

All of that is scary. But clinging to your illusion of control isn't bringing you peace, either. Ultimately, God wants to do more in your life than just ask you to let go. He wants to use your situation to strengthen you in His hope and shine His glory through your life.

Surrender is truly the path of peace, but only if you want it to be.

Think about a situation you've been worrying about or trying to fix without success. Here are three questions you can ask yourself about whether or not it's time to let go of control and surrender:

- Are you tired of trying to fix problems that aren't in your control?

Letting go means you have to admit you aren't in control and stop trying to act like God in others' lives.

- Are you tired of trying to fix people who don't want to do what is healthy or helpful for themselves?
- Are you tired of playing God?

If you've answered yes to any of these questions, then God is inviting you to hand over your control-loving remote control. It's hard, but you can do it!

Even if you aren't ready to surrender in this moment, take one step by reading this sneak peek of how God wants to bless you when you let go and let God transform your life.

If you let go of your fear,
God will give you FAITH.

If you let go of your "not enough,"
God will release His ABUNDANCE.
If you let go of your panic,
God will give you PEACE.
If you let go of your expectations,
God will give you the EXTRAORDINARY.
If you let go of your hurt,
God will give you HEALING.
If you let go of your guilt and shame,
God will give you GRACE.
If you let go of failure,
God will give you FORGIVENESS.
If you let go of your pain,
God will give you PURPOSE.

- What do you fear will happen if you stop trying to control a particular person or situation?
- Which one of the blessings above do you need most?

PRAYER: Dear God, I am tired of trying to fix/solve ________________. So today, I surrender myself and my situation over to You. Over these forty days, I commit to learning what it means to walk in surrender. Thank You for taking care of me and what I can't control. Amen.

Surrender Principle

I am not in control of others or outcomes.

SECTION II

Letting Go of Circumstances

Letting Go of Your Fear of "Not Enough"

"For your Father knows what you need before you ask him."
(Matthew 6:8b)

Do you realize that God knows how much you have in your bank and retirement accounts, how much is in your freezer and kitchen cabinets? He even knows about that secret bag of chocolate tucked away in its hiding place! Likewise, God knows exactly what you need to cover your mortgage, prescriptions, kids' tuition, and living expenses—now or in retirement. He knows it down to the last penny.

While we know that God knows it all, that doesn't stop us from fearing the "not enough" gaps that show up in our lives. Embedded deep into the DNA of our human nature is choosing fear and forgetting God's faithfulness, especially when the edges of what we have and what we need don't meet.

This "not enough" gap in your life is exactly where God wants to eliminate your fear and replace it with faith. These gaps are where you'll get to experience the miracle of more! You get to see more of God's power, presence, and provision in your life.

Long ago, the Israelites fled from Egypt in a blazing trail of divine miracles and through the heavenly parting of the Red Sea's deep waters. However, they were in the desert only for a short period of time before they began to panic about not having enough food and water.

God showed up in their gap. Not just once or twice. For forty years, the Israelites experienced the daily manna miracle in the wilderness (see Exodus 16). They didn't have a grocery store or paycheck, yet God provided because that's what He promised He would do.

For more than 14,600 days, God showed up and filled their "not enough" gap with a manna miracle. They had reminder after reminder. God provided what they needed for as long as they needed it.

The manna miracle was never about the manna. Rather, that daily miracle "reminds us that God may provide from resources that we never knew existed."[1] God provides for you because He has promised to provide and has the power to get it done.

God is never limited by what you lack. You don't need to have a job, a bank account, or even insurance. As I wrote in my *Surrendered* Bible study, "God takes care of His children at all times, especially hard times."[2] In other words, God meets us in our circumstances and provides for our needs regardless of the resources we have or anticipate.

Thousands of years later, Jesus taught the people the same principles of those ancient manna miracles. In Matthew 6:11, Jesus told His disciples to pray "give us today our daily bread," again calling them to expect and trust God to provide what they needed for each day. A few verses later, Jesus used flowers and birds as reminders that if God takes care of lesser creations, then how much more will God take care of human beings, who are made in His image?

Look at the drawing below and visualize whatever situation you're facing today. For whatever you lack, God's power, presence, promises, and provision are the 4 Ps that fill all of the "not enough" spaces in your life ("what you need"). Releasing your fear of "not enough" begins with acknowledging that God is enough, regardless of what you have or what you need. As my friend, the late Jennifer Dean wrote, "When we find Him, we find everything."[3]

What You Have | **God** | **What You Need**

- What are some of the gaps that you're dealing with today?
- What are some of the manna miracles pointing to God's power and provision in your life?

PRAYER: God, thank You for all of the times You've taken care of me and filled in the gaps. Today, I trust that You are enough for everything I need. Amen.

Surrender Principle

Trusting God's promises will bless me, but pushing my plans will stress me.

---

1. David Guzik, "Exodus 16—Manna for the Children of Israel," Enduring Word, 2018, https://enduringword.com/bible-commentary/exodus-16/.
2. Barb Roose, *Surrendered: Letting Go & Living Like Jesus* (Nashville: Abingdon Press, 2020), 23.
3. Jennifer Kennedy Dean, *Live a Praying Life: Open Your Life to God's Power and Provision* (Birmingham: New Hope, 2011), 121.

DAY 5

Letting Go of Worrying

Give all your worries and cares to God, for he cares about you. (1 Peter 5:7 NLT)

Do you ever make up stories in your mind about what will happen if you don't try to fix everything? Sometimes, our worries create a story line that develops into an awful mental movie, capturing our worst fears about what could happen.

In my *Joshua* Bible study, I call those negative mental movies WorryFlix.[1] While you never get billed for WorryFlix, watching it is very costly. Like your favorite streaming-video service, WorryFlix serves up episode after episode of unhappy endings to whatever problem you or a loved one is facing. If you watch enough WorryFlix each day, you're likely to be worn out, discouraged, and feeling pretty desperate.

Worn out. Discouraged. Desperate. That describes how the Israelites felt after escaping Egypt. They'd been in the wilderness a short time when a lack of food created a panic among the people. They didn't need sophisticated technology to play their own mental movies of running out of food or water in the wilderness. However, their WorryFlix was wearing them out.

Are you worn out?

Letting go of worry means that you believe God is *with* you and *for* you in every circumstance of your life. As Romans 8:31 says, "If God is for us, who can be against us?" You can cancel your WorryFlix subscription by choosing to visualize GodFlix, which is a mental movie that plays episodes starring God's promises for your life. While GodFlix doesn't mean that your

Letting go of worry means that you believe God is with you and for you in every circumstance of your life.

life is perfect or problem-free, you see yourself or your loved ones in God's presence, experiencing His power and resting in His provision.

How do you cancel that WorryFlix subscription? First Peter 5:7 offers helpful instructions for a powerful remove-and-replace operation when it comes to letting go of worry.

First, you're instructed to take action and give to God. To give means that you have to let go. You can't give and keep at the same time.

Second, you have to round up *all* of your worries and give them to God. Too often, we like to hold onto a few that we think that we can still fix: "God, I'll give you my worries about my job and my health, but I'm going to try to keep fixing my finances." Using a different metaphor, worry is like black mold. If you hold onto one or two worries, all of your worry problems will grow back!

Third, when you let go of worry, remember that God cares about you. He wants what is best for you!

God knows that worry wears you out. So, when you give your worries to God, then you can focus on Him, remember His promises, and enjoy the blessings He brings into your life every day.

- What worries and cares do you need to give to God today?

- Are there one or two worries that are hard for you to give up? Why?

PRAYER: Dear God, I need to let go of my worry! I'm tired of being worn out by WorryFlix whenever I think about what I can't control. Today, I'm giving to You all of my worries and cares about _______________ and _______________ and _______________. Instead of worrying about what will happen, I will focus on Your promises and remember that You care about me and everyone I love. In Jesus' name. Amen.

Surrender Principle

I can always let go and give my problems to God.

---

1. Barb Roose, *Joshua: Winning the Worry Battle* (Nashville: Abingdon Press, 2018), 73.

DAY 6

Letting Go of Fixing

Trust in the Lord *with all your heart*
and lean not on your own understanding.
(Proverbs 3:5)

How easy (or difficult) is it for you to accept what you can't change? You're not alone if acceptance feels like giving up, especially when you feel like you still have some ideas that just might work if you keep going.

Have you poured out all of the money, given all of the lectures, made all of the suggestions, or filled in all of the gaps—all with no success?

It's so hard to accept that there are some people and things you just can't fix.

Once upon a time, I fancied myself a Mrs. Fix-It. I took pride in my toolbox of ideas, plans, and strategies intended to rescue and repair others and outcomes. Part of my fixing philosophy was to strike quick in the moment to keep the person or problem from getting out of hand.

Here's what I discovered: First, people don't like to be fixed, and they'll often fight it. This dynamic causes conflict, which is always a clue that points to control-loving behaviors.

Second, fixing forces temporary Band-Aid solutions. Instead, we need to trust God to bring real hope and true healing in the future.

One of the aha moments during my surrender journey occurred when I discovered the difference between fixing and acting by faith.

> *Fixing* manifests itself through control-loving behaviors directed toward others.
>
> *Acting by faith* involves taking responsible actions for myself and allowing God to be in control of others.

So, what does it look like to let go of fixing and act by faith? Jesus demonstrated this for us in the garden of Gethsemane. After Jesus finished His anguished prayer to God, surrendering His life to God's will (Matthew 26:39-44), Judas arrived with a large crowd of armed men. Jesus knew that Judas

God can do more in an instant than you can do in a lifetime, and He doesn't need your help.

would betray Him and said, "Do what you came for, friend" (Matthew 26:50).

If there was ever a problem Jesus could have fixed Himself, this was it! Jesus could have taken Himself out of that situation like He had done at other times (Luke 4:30, John 10:39). Jesus could have left town and fled. He could have nagged Judas until the traitor and his crowd of men backed off.

Yet, Jesus didn't do any of those things. He didn't try to manipulate the moment; instead, He stayed focused on God's best for the future, even if that meant experiencing pain in the present.

God can do more in an instant than you can do in a lifetime, and He doesn't need your help. When you feel compelled to problem-solve, ask yourself, "Am I trying to fix this to make me feel better now, or do I need to stand in faith and let God handle it?" Letting go of fixing can be summed up in this declaration: *If it's gonna get done, then God's gonna have to do it.* Do you need to look at your situation and say this today?

- In your efforts to fix, what damage have you created in your relationships?
- How can you substitute faith for fixing in that situation?

PRAYER: Dear God, today I need to let go of trying to fix ________. I have tried so hard to make it better, but I can see that this is a problem I can't fix. So God, today, I will let go of trying to fix and use control-loving behaviors. I choose to believe that if it's gonna get done, You're gonna have to do it! I trust in You. In Jesus' name. Amen.

Surrender Principle

I can always let go and give my problems to God.

DAY 7

Letting Go of Overthinking

And now, dear brothers and sisters, one final thing.
Fix your thoughts on what is true, and honorable,
and right, and pure, and lovely, and admirable.
Think about things that are excellent and worthy of praise.
(Philippians 4:8 NLT)

Do you keep spinning a wheel of mental options like you're a contestant on a television game show? For every option, you consider all sides over and over again. You turn every possibility upside down and around. Yet, even when you're 100 percent sure of what you should do, you can't stop yourself from giving the wheel another spin. *What if I'm missing something...*

I asked a few friends what overthinking felt like to them:

> "There are times when I am paralyzed by indecision and anxiety."

> "Right now, I'm overthinking while packing for my trip. What to wear? What if I'm underdressed? What if I'm overdressed? What if I get cold?"

Overthinking happens when we're searching for the pain-free or problem-free path to the outcome that we want. However, overthinking often leads to feeling overwhelmed because we feel like 100 percent of the responsibility depends on us.

When you're constantly spinning that wheel of options, do you feel at peace or do you feel overwhelmed by a list of endless problems?

Letting go of overthinking means making God-honoring choices confidently and living by faith that God will help you deal with consequences. Years ago, I heard some wisdom that freed me from spinning my wheel of options: "Don't make the right decision; make the decision right."[1]

So, what do you do with your wheel of options? Replace it with a Wheel of Peace. Philippians 4:8 lists eight qualities that bring peace into your mind instead of panic. When you spin the Wheel of Peace and meditate on God's thoughts, that discipline will guard your heart and mind and keep you in alignment with God's heart toward you.

Let's practice spinning the Wheel of Peace. Put your finger on one of the eight characteristics on the wheel to select it, and then mediate on the corresponding statement below:

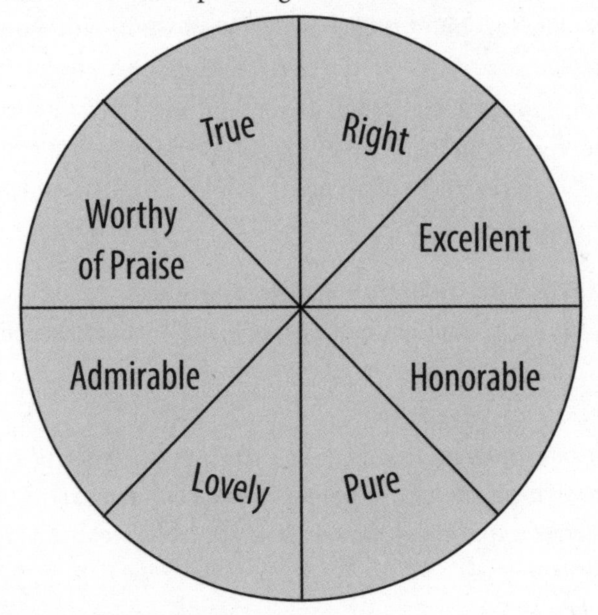

TRUE: God is with me and for me.

RIGHT: I am blessed when I do life God's way, not my own.

EXCELLENT: I desire a pure heart and godly actions.

HONORABLE: I will treat myself and others with respect, even when it's hard.

PURE: I might be struggling, but I can always ask God for His strength.

LOVELY: God's beauty is all around me, and I choose to see it.

ADMIRABLE: I believe that God isn't done blessing me!

WORTHY OF PRAISE: I will look for what's good and give thanks for what God is doing in my life.

If there were ever anything *good* to overthink, try overthinking God's blessings and love for you. Seriously, try it! You know what it's like to "spin" on uncontrollable situations and negative outcomes; now "spin" for the same amount of time on God's provisions for you, His promises for you, and His love for you. The more you spin the Wheel of Peace, the more peace you will experience in the midst of whatever problem, trial, or wilderness season you are facing.

- What decisions do you often overthink?
- What quality in the Wheel of Peace encourages you today?

PRAYER: God, I think way too much. I need to spin Your Wheel of Peace. I will take my focus off trying to figure everything out, and I will rely upon what I know is true about You and how You feel about me. In Jesus' name. Amen.

Surrender Principle

Surrender is my only path to God's peace.

1. Ellen Langer, *Mindfulness: 25th Anniversary Edition* (Boston: Da Capo, 2014), 198.

DAY 8

Letting Go of Negative Thinking

I trust in God's unfailing love
for ever and ever.
(Psalm 52:8b)

You'd think that the Israelites' memories would have lasted much longer. After all, God had freed them from slavery in dramatic fashion, split the Red Sea, and eliminated their enemies, the Egyptians.

However, only a short time later, the Israelites questioned God's plan. Instead of believing the best about God, they chose to think the worst.

> *"If only the Lord had killed us back in Egypt," they moaned. "There we sat around pots filled with meat and ate all the*

> *bread we wanted. But now you have brought us into this wilderness to starve us all to death."*
>
> *(Exodus 16:3 NLT)*

So, *that's* how they remembered life in Egypt? They remembered the food, but they'd forgotten about the slavery, oppression, beatings, and murder of their infant sons? Once they were in the wilderness and couldn't control their circumstances, the Israelites allowed their perspective to become pessimistic.

When you can't control your circumstances, does your thinking become more negative or more positive? Unfortunately, control-loving behaviors plus negative thinking create a kind of control loop we can get stuck in. We control because we're afraid, and when we're afraid, we resort to trying to control.

**We control because we're afraid,
and when we're afraid,
we resort to trying to control.**

Letting go of negative thoughts is a challenge because those thoughts are like toxic bodybuilders. When you look for the negative, you're going to find it every time. Then, those negative thoughts grow stronger and more powerful the more you feed them. Negative thoughts are noisy and rude, ruining your chance to enjoy God's blessings and the kindness of others.

You can let go of negative thinking by introducing something stronger than your negative thoughts. It begins with fully embracing the reality and power of God's love. For some of us, trusting in God doesn't come to us naturally. In fact, Paul prayed that we'd "grasp how wide and long and high and deep is the love of Christ, and to know this love that surpasses knowledge—that you may be filled to the measure of all the fullness of God" (Ephesians 3:18*b*-19).

In Psalm 52, David was upset and angry because his enemies wouldn't leave him alone. Yet, rather than settle into an Eeyore-like mentality and assume the worst, David believed the best about God. In verse 8*b*, he proclaimed, "I trust in God's unfailing love / forever and ever" and experienced the perfect love that casts out fear (1 John 4:18).

You can too. Rather than believe the worst about yourself or your situation, believe that God loves you completely! His love for you holds you in the midst of, comforts you in spite of, and heals you from any loss or pain you might face. When you are fully and continually convinced of the fullness of God's love, there's no room for negative thoughts in your heart or mind. If a negative thought does pop up, just pour the truth of God's love on it, and that love will cancel your negative thoughts or fears.

- What are some negative thoughts that persist in your heart or mind?
- Compare your negative thoughts to the evidence of God's love for you. What does that comparison reveal?

PRAYER: Dear God, You really do love me and care about me. God, I'm so sorry for all of the negative thoughts I've allowed to grow too strong in my mind. I will trust in Your unfailing love for me and spend more time focusing on what I'm grateful for instead of grumbling about what I don't have. Amen.

Surrender Principle

I can always let go and give my problems to God.

DAY 9

Letting Go of Interrupting

Everyone should be quick to listen,
slow to speak and slow to become angry.
(James 1:19b)

Three-year-old Mateo Beltran really wanted some cupcakes, and his mother said no. Unfortunately, he did not like her answer. After a video that went viral on social media a number of years ago, little Mateo became better known as the little boy who said, "Listen, Linda" over and over again.[1] While little Mateo's interruptions are funny in the video, regularly interrupting others is no laughing matter.

Here are two ways that we can use interrupting as a control-loving behavior:

- when we cut someone off while they are talking
- when we interfere in another's affairs

If you're like me, you don't mean to interrupt others. In fact, you truly believe that what you are saying or doing will make the situation better. For instance, when someone is telling a story and I jump in, it's because I want to add to the laughter and fun in the moment. If my kids are telling me about a problem and I jump in before they finish talking, it's because I want to hurry them along toward solving their problem and feeling less stress.

Did you notice that the letter *I* begins the word *interrupting*? That is so telling! My interruptions often reveal a desire to push a self-centered priority of *me* over the precious relational connection of *we*.

In Luke 10, Martha welcomed Jesus and the disciples into her home. With a crowd of hungry men, Martha was probably feeling some serious stress and pressure to be hospitable to her guests. However, she was upset with her sister, Mary, for not jumping in and helping. In fact, Martha went to Jesus and asked him to tell Mary to help Martha.

I love Jesus' response to Martha: "My dear Martha, you are worried and upset over all these details! [42]There is only one thing worth being concerned about. Mary has discovered it, and it will not be taken away from her" (Luke 10:41-42 NLT).

The core motive for interruption begins with *I* and is focused on self. Martha wanted to interrupt Mary's agenda because Martha believed

Letting go of interrupting means stepping back in the moment and taking the focus off of ourselves before we push our agenda, our words, or our demands on others.

her own agenda was more important. Jesus wasn't angry when he corrected Martha, but He let her know that Mary was doing exactly what was right for her in that moment, and He wasn't going to interrupt Mary because of Martha's pressing desires.

Letting go of interrupting means stepping back in the moment and taking the focus off of ourselves before we push our agenda, our words, or our demands on others.

The best practical advice on letting go of interrupting comes from the priceless wisdom in James 1:19:

1. **Quick to listen**—Ask God to help you use your ears before you open your mouth.
2. **Slow to speak**—Make sure that your words don't dominate your conversations or undermine someone else's actions.
3. **Slow to get angry**—Practice humility and take the focus off of your feelings and the desire to get what you want.

- When do you interrupt others?
- In which of your relationships do you need to apply the wisdom of James 1:19?

PRAYER: Dear God, I can quickly get wrapped up in my excitement, agitation, or agenda and push it onto others. Help me take the focus off of myself and keep it on You, loving others in a way that honors You. In Jesus' name. Amen.

Surrender Principle

I am not in control of others or outcomes.

---

1. Alex Heigl, "'Listen, Listen, Linda!' Toddler's Skillful Debate Goes Viral," *People*, March 18, 2014, https://people.com/celebrity/mateo-beltran-listen-linda-listen-debate-with-mom-over-cupcakes-goes-viral/.

DAY 10

Letting Go of Mistakes

Therefore, there is now no condemnation
for those who are in Christ Jesus.
(Romans 8:1)

A few days into our long-awaited family cruise, I couldn't find an envelope that contained a single, crisp $100 bill. A tiny panic flamed in the pit of my stomach. *Oh, no!*

I ransacked our stateroom. Then, I realized that I might have thrown the envelope into the trash the day before. I felt sick. In our home, we banned the word *stupid*, but you can bet I had broken the world record for using it because I kept whispering it to myself over and over again.

My mistake cost our family something. While they didn't care, I felt like I should pay a price. So I felt the only way to make up for my mistake was to punish myself with critical and shaming words.

Are you the type of person who makes a mistake and apologizes but doesn't feel truly remorseful unless you keep beating yourself up over and over again?

In the New Testament, Peter is the most outspoken of Jesus' disciples. In fact, on one occasion Peter declares himself more faithful than Jesus' other disciples (Matthew 26:33). Later, Peter feels great pain and shame after he denies knowing Jesus on three separate occasions (Luke 22:54-62).

Perhaps, you know how Peter feels. You can't rest because you failed big or dropped the ball, and you can't let it go. Whether intentional or not, you think beating yourself up is the price you must pay for what you've done. However, Romans 8:1 is proof that God isn't beating you up. *You are.*

Letting go of your mistakes gives you an opportunity to experience the miracle of restoration and grace. Because of Jesus' death and resurrection, your mistakes are not the measuring stick of your life. Your mistakes may be part of your life story, but they can also become a message that demonstrates God's glory and grace to others.

Lucky for Peter, he saw Jesus shortly after the resurrection (Luke 24:34), and in John 21, Jesus restored Peter again to ministry.

Now, imagine how Peter felt as he lay his head down that night. He not only felt the lightness of forgiveness but also knew that his past mistake wouldn't keep him from future opportunities to make a difference.

Jesus died to free you from the guilt, shame, and condemnation we all face at one point or another. We are human, but thankfully our humanness isn't a problem for God. I often think of this quote, attributed to Lisa Bevere: "If you think you've blown God's plan for your life, rest in this. You, my friend, are not that powerful."

Is today the day you will stop calling yourself a mistake, a failure, a waste, or something worse? Give yourself a gift by reading Romans 8:1 (page 41) and today's prayer below:

PRAYER: Dear God, I am so tired of feeling the guilt and shame of ________________ (a mistake). Thank You that Jesus died for me so that I can lay my head down at night in the assurance that my mistakes are not the measure of who I am. Thank You that Jesus died for me so that I can wake up and live each day in the joy of Your grace and mercy in my life. In Jesus' name. Amen.

Surrender Principle

Surrender is my only path to God's peace.

Letting Go of the Past

But I focus on this one thing: Forgetting the past and looking forward to what lies ahead. (Philippians 3:13b NLT)

Our dog, Quimby, is the best forgetter ever. Even though she was abused before she came to live with us, Quimby wakes up each day happily wagging her tail and licking our faces. She never remembers when we yelled at her the day before. For Quimby, each day is a clean slate. I wish I could be a lot more like my dog.

For humans, it's not easy to forget the past. We're prone to negative bias, and it's much easier to remember the bad instead of the good. We tend to drag the past with us like suitcases into and out of our jobs, relationships, and dreams. Packed in those

You can carry your past around for only so long before it begins to cost you.

suitcases are our disappointments, pain, missed opportunities, expectations, abandonment, rejections, and failures.

You can carry your past around for only so long before it begins to cost you. The more suitcases you have, the more your past slows you down, messes you up, and keeps you stuck and unable to experience God's very best for your life.

In Philippians 3, the apostle Paul wrote about the joy of being freed from his past. Paul wasn't just freed from the sin; he experienced the fullness of God's peace, hope, joy, purpose, and abundance in his life in spite of his past.

Forgetting your past doesn't mean you live in denial or get amnesia. God wants to apply His healing power to your past and free you from carrying the weight of it in and out of your relationships, your hopes, and your dreams. Who you are *now* in Christ is far more important than what you've done or what was done to you in the past.

How do you ask God to disconnect your past from influencing your life now? I use a tool I call my "annual funeral." I've used it for more than a decade and wrote about it in my Bible study, *I'm Waiting, God.*[1] This experience puts me in position for God to help me let go of my past. I grab my Bible and journal and go to a quiet place where I can think, cry, and pray. Here's how you can do this too.

Step 1: Be Real with God

Tell God about all of your painful memories, unmet expectations, resentments, and disappointments in your life.

Step 2: Write It Down

Writing down everything you're pouring out to God makes your feelings, emotions, and perspective real. Recording these not only acknowledges everything that you've been holding in but also symbolically lets it out.

Step 3: Release

This final step is a surrender prayer in which you acknowledge everything from your past that hurt you.

- What part of your past is hard to let go of?
- Imagine what life might be like if you let go of your past. What's one next step you can take today toward letting go?

PRAYER: Dear God, would You free me from the weight of ________ from my past? I've tried to fix and forget what's happened, but I can't do it on my own. I'm praying for Your mighty power to release me from what I've been dragging all this time. It's hurting me. I know Your power can deliver me and bring me to the promised place of Your perfect peace and blessing. In Jesus' name. Amen.

Surrender Principle

Surrender is my only path to God's peace.

---

1. Barb Roose, *I'm Waiting, God: Finding Blessing in God's Delays* (Nashville: Abingdon Press, 2019), 119

DAY 12

Letting Go of Pacifiers

"Man shall not live on bread alone, but on every word that comes from the mouth of God."
(Matthew 4:4b)

When my daughter Sami was an infant, I placed six pacifiers around her crib at night. I wanted to make sure that if one fell out of her mouth, she could reach out and grab another without much effort.

However, pacifiers aren't just for kids.

What are you facing that makes you want to seek comfort? Maybe you long for your kids to make good decisions, for your health or finances to get straightened out, or for help caring for elderly parents.

When we're feeling uncomfortable and not getting what we want, it's easy for us to find a pacifier to soothe unsettled emotions, unhealed pain, or sharp disappointments. Pacifiers come in different shapes and sizes. Some of us reach for comfort food, indulge in retail therapy, binge watch to numb out, overthink, engage in unhealthy sexual behaviors, or use addictive substances.

Pacifiers won't give us lasting satisfaction, only temporary and empty distraction. Yet, your pacifier is a helpful indicator that you're struggling with something you can't control.

Here are three words that have helped me break my addiction to pacifiers: *Only Jesus satisfies.*

Years ago, I used food as a pacifier. When I felt sad, I gravitated toward sweet and creamy foods. When I was stressed, I'd grab a Snickers bar. While each bite tasted good on my tongue, a million bites could never fill my aching soul.

Our souls must be *surrendered* to Christ before we can find *satisfaction* in Christ.

Satan understands how you feel. In Matthew 4, Satan tempted Jesus to use His divine powers to satisfy a human desire. *Jesus, you can fix your hunger right now if you turn those stones into bread.*

Rather than pick up a pacifier, Jesus showed us how to find satisfaction in God. He quoted Deuteronomy 8:3: "Man does not live on bread alone but on every word that comes from the mouth of the LORD."

Jesus knew His mission was to please God, not pacify human desires. The same goes for us. When we find satisfaction in God, we won't go looking for happiness anywhere else. The first step? Our souls must be *surrendered* to Christ before we can find *satisfaction* in Christ.

Jesus' example shows us how to use the power of God's words to fill our souls with peace. When I feel drawn to a pacifier, I write Matthew 4:4 on a Post-it note and stick it to one of my pacifiers. I'm reminding myself to seek God and not look for satisfaction anywhere else. When I'm stressed, God's words have power to fill me with lasting life and peace—without the weight gain.

Are there some pacifiers in your life that you have been using to fill an emotional or spiritual hunger? Your first step to victory is to surrender to God the space that you're trying to fill with a pacifier.

- What pacifiers do you turn to when you're stressed or feeling out of control?
- Do you sense something God wants you to do differently?

PRAYER: Dear God, I want You to be all I need. Today, I want to lay down anything or anyone I've put before You. While I know You invite me to pray to You about what's going on in my life, I don't want my desires to become more important than my desire for You. In Jesus' name. Amen.

Surrender Principle

I choose to live by faith,
not rush to follow my feelings.

DAY 13

Letting Go of Temptation

No temptation has overtaken you except what is common to mankind. And God is faithful; he will not let you be tempted beyond what you can bear. But when you are tempted, he will also provide a way out so that you can endure it.
(1 Corinthians 10:13)

Do you and your friends ever sit around and talk about temptation? Sometimes we might joke about feeling tempted to spend too much on a new purse or eat that extra piece of cake. However, our stories tend to fade to silence because we're often too afraid or ashamed to talk about the real temptations that threaten our health, our families, our finances, or most importantly, our faith.

It's not a sin to be tempted. At its essence, a temptation is an invitation to do something that would distract or derail our pursuit of God. Yet, God will never tempt us to sin (James 1:13). We often blame our temptation on a person, place, or thing. But the truth is temptation is an internal and spiritual struggle that reveals where we may not trust God's heart toward us.

We all face temptation. Unfortunately, we don't like to talk about it; we're not comfortable when others are courageous enough to talk about their temptations. In that awkward space, Satan will use a secret to stir up shame, and that shame can ruin your life.

While Jesus was in the wilderness, He faced three temptations we can all identify with today:

- temptation to use His divine power to satisfy a physical need
- temptation to avoid suffering and control God's timing
- temptation to be powerful and worshipped

While the Gospel writers didn't record every day of Jesus' life, God inspired them to include Jesus' time of temptation in the wilderness. Just think, God could have left out this particular event. However, God wanted us to know we're not alone when it comes to the siren song of temptation in our lives. In fact, Hebrews 4:15 tells us that Jesus was tempted in every way, but

Just as the Holy Spirit was with Jesus in the wilderness, God's Holy Spirit is with you in those wilderness moments too.

He didn't sin. So whatever temptation you're facing today, don't believe Satan's lie that no one will understand! You can talk to Jesus about it!

Without a doubt, Satan seeks to destroy your life (John 10:10). He will dangle that juicy bit of gossip, the house that's too expensive, or that inappropriate relationship to draw you away from God. But just as the Holy Spirit was with Jesus in the wilderness, God's Holy Spirit is with you in those wilderness moments too. You have the power to stand against temptation. On the other side of temptation, you stand in victory and celebrate as an overcomer. Satan may try to overwhelm you, but in Jesus' name, you will rise up as an overcomer! As Ralph Waldo

Emerson observed, "We gain the strength of the temptation we resist."[1]

- What are some temptations that you don't like to talk about?
- What temptation do you need to confess to a safe and trusted person?

PRAYER: God, today I am fighting the temptation to ___________. Rather than blame the object of my temptation, I admit that I am struggling to trust You in _______________ [area of my life]. Give me the courage to confess my temptation to a trusted friend today. I am ready to take this first step toward freedom, healing, and victory. In Jesus' name. Amen!

Surrender Principle

I choose to live by faith,
not rush to follow my feelings.

1. Ralph Waldo Emerson: *Essays and Lectures* (New York: Library of America, 1983), 298.

DAY 14

Letting Go of the Future

"For I know the plans I have for you," declares the LORD, "plans to prosper you and not to harm you, plans to give you hope and a future." *(Jeremiah 29:11)*

We like happy endings.

During the difficult years of the Great Depression and World War II, Hollywood movie directors rewrote the endings to popular books such as *The Grapes of Wrath* to have happy movie endings. Since there was so much sadness around the war, the movie studios wanted to create a cinematic happy ending, even if the books didn't end that way. One article called this revisionist process "happyendingification" or the taking of a bad situation and turning it into a happy one.[1]

Do you ever try to do some "happyendingification" in your life? When we or someone we love is struggling or when a situation we hate is out of control, we grab our control-loving remote to point and click our way to an ending in which everyone is smiling and happy when the final credits roll.

However, we don't watch movies just because we want to see the end. The unfolding story line draws us in. Watching the characters face tragedies and triumph over their personal problems makes for a rich and full story. The ending is only part of the experience.

The same goes for you. While you might be fixated on creating a happy ending, God wants to change your heart along the way. His ultimate plans for you include making you more like Christ. God is more concerned with your character than your comfort.

I spent years trying to force happy endings in my life. I thought that if I worked hard enough and long enough, I could make those happy endings happen. Yet, even as I tried to control my way to a happy ending, my control-loving behaviors piled up fear, frustration, and damaged relationships in my everyday life.

You can't control what will happen in the future, but you can trust God here and now. Let God's promises, not your plans, direct your hopes and dreams. When you let go of your view of how the future should look, you're free to see the possibilities through God's promises, not just your perspective.

God's plan for the beginning, middle, and end of your life will bless you when you trust Him. Jeremiah 29:11 reminds us that God has more for us because God has put more in us. So, when God says that He has a plan, you can be certain that God can handle everything, even if you can't.

One of the treasures I've learned in my surrender journey is this: God is my future. He is my outcome.

The same is true for you. God is your future. He is your outcome.

God knows your story line from the beginning to the middle and the end, and you can be certain He knows how to end the story well.

- What are some of the bad endings you fear?
- When you consider that God is your future, how does that shift your perspective on whatever you're facing today?

PRAYER: Dear God, You are my future! Today, I need to let go of the future I want to see in regard to ____________________ and focus my eyes on You. I trust that Your presence, Your promises, and Your provision will be all I need. In Jesus' name. Amen.

Surrender Principle

Surrender is my only path to God's peace.

---

1. Finlo Rohrer, "Why the Obsession with Happy Endings?" *BBC News Magazine*, April 1, 2009, http://news.bbc.co.uk/2/hi/uk_news/magazine/7976192.stm.

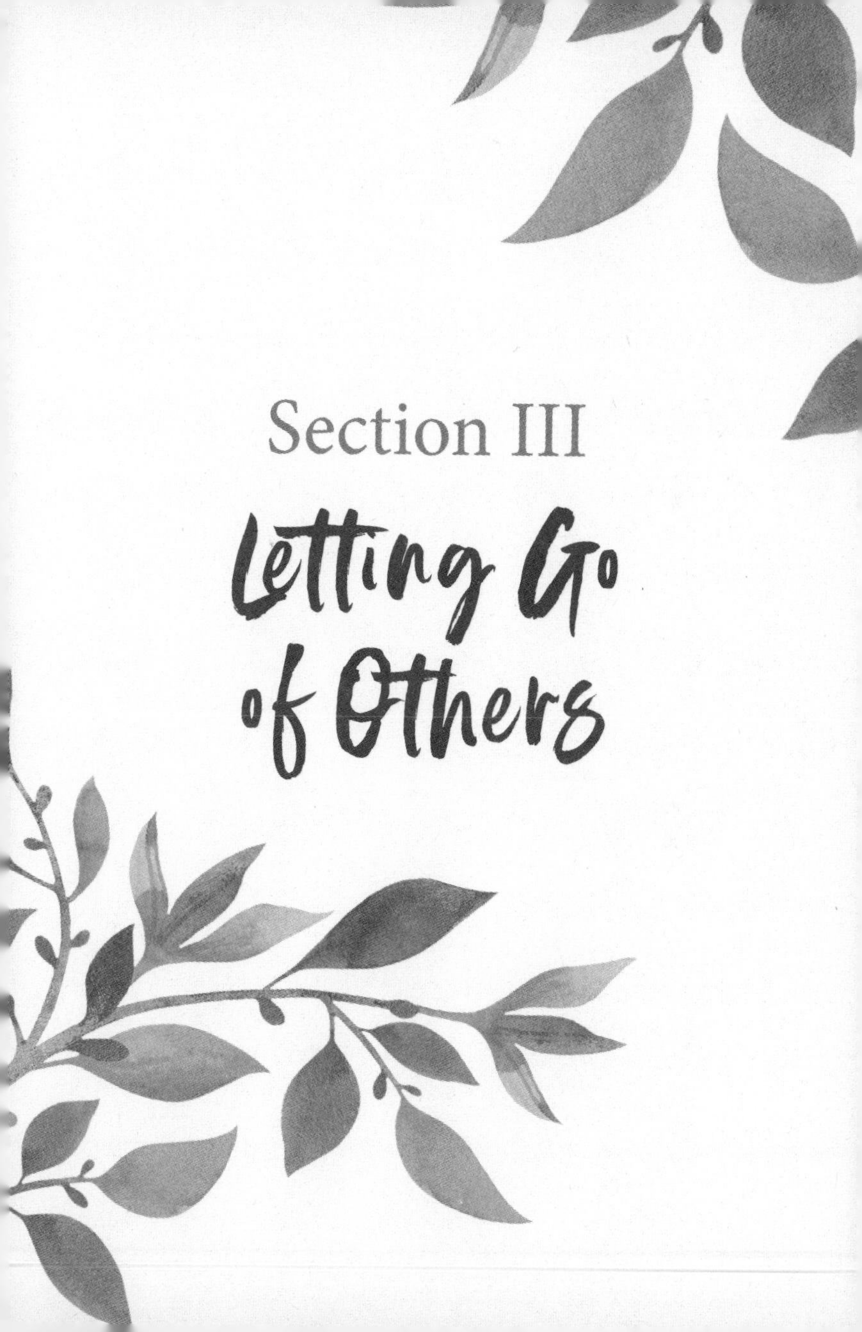

Section III

Letting Go of Others

DAY 15

Letting Go of Nagging

The tongue has the power of life and death.
(Proverbs 18:21a)

I'm a descendant from a long line of well-meaning women whose nagging is a preferred expression of love. You can calculate just how much you're loved based on the number of times we call or text you, reminding you to wear your coat, take your medicine, or phone when you get home.

Perhaps you're feeling like you could be a part of my family because you love to repeat requests and recap instructions or dire warnings to your loved ones. If so, welcome to my family. I'm glad you're here!

For our first family meeting, we're going to talk about why the people we love don't feel loved by our repetitious words.

Proverbs 18:21 teaches that the power of life and death is in our words. In fact, the Book of Proverbs contains multiple verses that point to nagging as a destructive way of using our words. It's actually a control-loving behavior that wears down our relationships. In fact, the origin of the word *nag* is "to gnaw."[1]

Most of the time, our repeating words come from our desire to protect what we love, fix what's broken, or keep things on track. We can't or don't see how our nagging words gnaw at the precious fabric of our connections. God wants us to love people, but it isn't our job to save them.

Jesus used a lot of words to teach people, but He never used His words to nag. Think of all of the people Jesus met or the disciples who traveled with Jesus. Since He knew about all of the sin in their lives, Jesus could have nagged Peter to stop being so impulsive or Judas to stop stealing from their group treasury. Yet, Jesus taught truth to the people, connected with His disciples, and let everyone choose how they wanted to live.

In one instance, when Jesus was leaving to get away from the crowds in Matthew 8, one man asked Jesus to wait for him to bury his father. Jesus replied, "Follow me, and let the dead bury their own dead" (Matthew 8:22).

Jesus wasn't telling the man to abandon his father; rather, Jesus wanted to clarify the man's priorities. After that conversation,

God wants us to love people, but it isn't our job to save them.

Jesus didn't run after the man and remind him. In our time, He wouldn't text the man once a day to ask *Hey, are you coming?* Jesus told the man what he needed to do and then let the man live with the consequences of his choice.

Letting go of nagging means that we say what we need to say once and let people live with the consequences of what they do next.

Here's the bottom line when it comes to letting go of nagging: saying it once is telling; repeating it more than once is nagging. Before you open your mouth, ask yourself if you need to repeat what you're going to say or if you should pray to God about it instead?

- If you nag, what fears are behind those repetitious words?
- How can you surrender these fears to God instead of nagging others?

PRAYER: Dear God, it's so hard to stop nagging! You know how much I love the people in my life and how much I want what is best for them. Yet, God, I have to remember that You love them even more! Please convict my heart. I don't want to gnaw away at my precious relationships. Remind me to come near to You in prayer instead of nagging away at those I love. In Jesus' name. Amen.

Surrender Principle

When fear tempts me to flee, fix, or force my way, I will choose to stop and pray.

1. *Online Etymology Dictionary*, s.v. "nag (v.)," accessed June 9, 2020, www.etymonline.com/word/nag.

DAY 16

Letting Go of Struggling Adult Children

"Not long after that, the younger son got together all he had, set off for a distant country and there squandered his wealth in wild living."
(Luke 15:13)

At first, you thought your son or daughter was just going through a hard time. Then, you told yourself that they were just rebelling, but they'd grow out of it. Yet, over the years, they've lied to you and you've listened to excuse after excuse about job-hopping, unemployment, or jail time. You've worn yourself and your finances out, wondering whether or not they would get it together.

Every single one of us was a spiritual prodigal at one point.

What do we do when we can't protect our adult children from themselves? How do we stand by when we can't fix them, no matter how badly we beg, bargain, or bully them? How many prayers have we prayed, begging God to help them get their lives back on track?

Jesus tells a story illustrating the lengths to which God goes to save His lost children, and in it are several precious nuggets that provide help and hope for you in the midst of what you and your struggling adult child are going through.

In Luke 15, Jesus begins his story with a son who demands what he is due to receive after his father dies. However, his father is still alive. *Son, are you telling me that you want me to cash out your inheritance now, before I'm even gone?*

Can you imagine the father's heartache? Regardless, the father gives the son his inheritance, and the son leaves home. While this is a fictional story, a similar scenario may be real in your life.

In *Parents with Broken Hearts*, the author offers the hope that a parent needs: "The good news is that God will travel with our son or daughter. They won't be going alone. This is the true hope of every believing parent."[1]

As Jesus teaches a group of self-righteous religious leaders by sharing the story of the prodigal son, He provides three pieces of wisdom that equip us to surrender our adult children to God.

1. The father didn't chase the son. He stayed home. (Luke 15:12–13, 20)
2. The son had to make the decision to turn his life around (Luke 15:18).
3. When the son came home, the father celebrated his son instead of criticizing him (Luke 15:22).

Every single one of us was a spiritual prodigal at one point. All of us. God lets the evidence of His love show all around us, but He never demands or forces us to come home to Him. Salvation is a personal decision to repent and turn to God. We have to make that decision on our own.

The same goes for our adult children. All of your begging, bargaining, and bullying might temporarily change their behavior, but not their hearts. That will only happen when they surrender to God. When He transforms their hearts, then their lives will change.

- How has not letting go of your adult child's struggle created hardship for you?
- In light of Jesus' teaching, what wisdom can you apply to your situation today?

PRAYER: Dear God, today I am taking the first step of surrendering [name] __________________ to You. To let go, I need to stop __________________ in hopes of trying to save them. I need to trust that You are present and active in their life. In Jesus' name. Amen.

Surrender Principle

Trusting God's promises will bless me, but pushing my plans will stress me.

1. William L. Coleman, *Parents with Broken Hearts: Helping Parents of Prodigals to Cope* (Winona Lake, IN: BMH Publishing, 1996), 29.

DAY 17

Letting Go of Helicoptering

A right time to hold on and another to let go.
(Ecclesiastes 3:6 MSG)

During a tense driving lesson, one of my daughters said, "Mom, please stop talking. I can't concentrate when you're always telling me stuff." I thought I was being helpful. My advice was intended to prevent her from hitting the curb or, worse yet, swerving into traffic. Secretly, I wished for a brake pedal on my side of the car so I could slam it to the floorboard to stop her from making a move that would hurt her or us.

Eventually, my daughter became so stressed out that she ended the driving lesson. As she pulled into a private driveway to turn around, she accidentally hit the gas pedal instead of the brake. We had a wild few seconds as the car launched across the drive into the middle of the home's front yard. Thankfully, she slammed on the brakes in time to stop the car right in front of the home's family room window.

As we sat in the silent car, I could feel my daughter's fury and frustration. At first, I thought, *Why is she upset? I was just trying to help!*

In reality, I'd opened up my control-loving toolbox and began interrupting and nagging at her to do it my way. My fears automatically assumed failure on her part, and I sabotaged an opportunity for her to figure it out on her own.

Helicoptering is a control-loving behavior that prompts us to micromanage others. We can helicopter our kids or our employees or even our elderly parents because we're afraid they won't get it right. We believe that the more help and advice we give, the less likely the person we care about will mess up.

Unfortunately, this isn't true. The more advice we give someone, the more frustrated and angry they usually become, especially when it's unsolicited advice. Helicoptering doesn't reduce our fear, and like other control-loving behaviors, it can wreck our relationships.

To let go of helicoptering, we need to recognize when it's time to stop being the gas and brake pedal in the lives of those we love and care about.

King Solomon captured this beautiful wisdom in Ecclesiastes 3:6, which says there is a "right time to hold on and another to let go." There is a time in life when we have to hold someone's hand and guide them step-by-step, but there's also a time when we've got to let go. We take a deep breath, pray, and then get out of the way.

Practically speaking, we say to others, "I know you will figure this out." We let them drive their life at their own pace without trying to hijack the journey, even when we're uncomfortable with the road that they're taking.

Letting go doesn't mean you don't love someone. In fact, it's actually a gift of respect. We can encourage instead of control.

- Who are you helicoptering these days, and what are you afraid of?
- How is letting go a gift?

PRAYER: Dear God, I have to trust You with ____________'s life/lives. I will trust that You are God in every single detail of their life, so I don't have to micromanage everything. I choose to let go and give ______________ a chance to discover that they need You and to experience the beauty of figuring life out on their own.

Surrender Principle

When fear tempts me to flee,
fix, or force my way,
I will choose to stop and pray.

DAY 18

Letting Go of a Broken Relationship

If it is possible, as far as it depends on you,
live at peace with everyone.
(Romans 12:18)

One day, I discovered that one of my favorite hoop earrings was missing. I wore them every day because they matched all of my outfits. I searched my room while wondering when the earring might have fallen out.

I held onto the remaining hoop for months in hopes that the missing hoop might turn up. While I had other earrings, that particular pair was important to me. I hated looking at that lonely earring in my jewelry box. I couldn't help thinking of how much I missed wearing them.

If you've ever experienced the loss of a friendship or a fallout with a family member, it's hard. Like a remaining earring, you come across lingering reminders that the special person is no longer a part of your life. Every time you remember that person, your heart aches because of the gaping space where that connection and that person used to be.

One of the most painful aspects of a broken relationship is the inability to repair the rift by yourself. You can't force someone to work things out with you. While forgiveness is an individual act of faith and obedience, reconciliation requires everyone involved to get engaged in the process. What happens when, despite all of your phone calls, prayers, and pleas, nothing happens and the rift remains? In that empty space where that

One of the most painful aspects of a broken relationship is the inability to repair the rift by yourself.

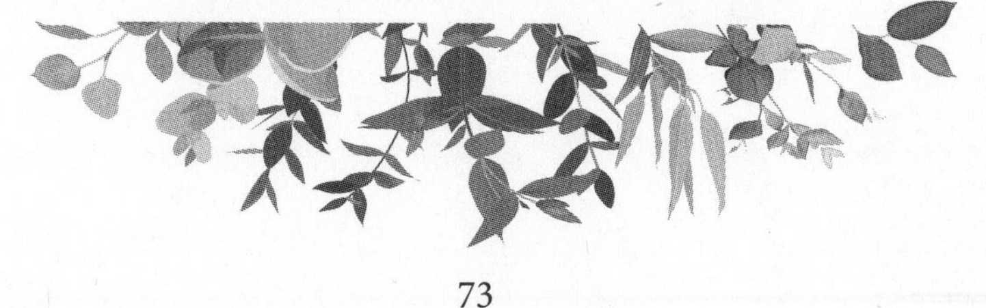

person used to be, you're left with memories, questions, and a lot of pain.

Within the wisdom of Romans 12:18 rests a few practical principles that define how God helps you live and learn to let go of a broken relationship so you can keep walking in peace, even if you're walking alone for now.

First, "if it is possible" implies that there will be times when reconciliation isn't possible. Just as Jesus had enemies who were out to hurt him, you may be dealing with someone who behaved badly and sought to hurt you purposely. Even though you miss them, you know they aren't safe until they repent or get help. You have permission to stay away from them, even if other well-meaning people try to guilt you into doing otherwise.

Second, "as far as it depends on you" means that you can only do so much to repair a broken relationship. You can nag someone, constantly text them, or even guilt them into sitting down and talking it out, but would your control-loving behaviors create a healthy beginning toward healing a broken relationship? Definitely not. The takeaway here is that God releases you from being wholly responsible for reconciliation.

Finally, "live at peace with everyone" means that you shouldn't stir the pot to keep the conflict going. No matter who is at fault, God is calling you to accept the painful situation as it is and leave it in His hands. When you live at peace, you experience the blessing and hope of God's promises no matter the outcome of that situation. Don't let that broken relationship steal your blessing!

In the meantime, keep praying for God's hand in healing and timing. While reconciliation is always God's goal, your responsibility is to forgive and be ready *if* reconciliation is an opportunity in the future.

- Is there a relationship in which you're stirring the pot and creating more conflict? Ask God to reveal this pattern in you.
- Which aspect of Romans 12:18 do you need to apply to a broken relationship?

PRAYER: God, it's so painful not having ____________________ as part of my life. But, it's not my responsibility to fix our relationship. I need to forgive (if needed) and be ready for the day that reconciliation may occur. In Jesus' name. Amen.

Surrender Principle

I am not in control of others or outcomes.

DAY 19

Letting Go of People-Pleasing

If I were still trying to please people,
I would not be a servant of Christ.
(Galatians 1:10b)

Do you tend to say yes or sure because you want people to like you or think you're kind, wonderful, and amazing? Or so you feel really good about yourself?

People-pleasing is actually a control-loving behavior with the goal of being liked. However, our desire to be liked by others can end up sabotaging our health, our life, and often, our faith.

Before he traveled to Mount Sinai, Moses left his brother, Aaron, and another man in charge. Soon, the newly freed Israelites began to wonder what happened to the guy who led them out of Egypt.

Ultimately, people-pleasing comes down to pursuing selfish glory instead of living for God's glory.

As temporary leader, Aaron said yes to helping the Israelites make a golden calf to worship, even though he knew that idol worship was God's biggest no-no. I wonder if Aaron said yes to get on others' good side or if he wanted to keep the complaint-prone crowd content.

As Moses came down from Mount Sinai, he saw the people worshipping the golden calf. After slamming his stone tablets to the ground, an angry Moses confronted Aaron, who shrugged his shoulders and said something like, "Well, you know how these people can be."

While each Israelite was responsible for his or her decision to worship the idol, Aaron's people-pleasing decision to say yes undermined God's command to worship Him alone.

Ultimately, people-pleasing comes down to pursuing selfish glory instead of living for God's glory. Galatians 1:10, therefore, suggests that letting go of people-pleasing begins with knowing where you need to say yes to God first. In my book *Winning the Worry Battle*, I define this by the four Cs:

> **Conviction:** What is my role at home or work in this season of my life?
> **Clarity:** What are the things that only I can do at home or in my job?
> **Creativity:** What are the unique gifts and talents that I want or need to use in this season of life?
> **Connection:** What relationship is God calling me to prioritize?[1]

It's not wrong to want people to think well of you, but it becomes a problem when that is your primary concern. What God thinks of you is what matters most. So, say yes to God first so that you're aligned with God's purpose for your life instead of following someone else's plan.

- When is people-pleasing a problem for you?
- Where do you need to say yes to God first?

PRAYER: God, I want to say yes to serving You rather than give my yeses to being liked by others.

Today, I want to acknowledge that I've been saying yes to __________________ because I want ____________________.

God, my people-pleasing yeses have meant that I've been saying no to the commands and convictions You've put on my heart, such as __________________.

As I pray, I sense that You are calling me to let go of my yes to __________________ so that I can love You with my heart, mind, body, and soul.

Give me the words to have those difficult conversations as well as the conviction to live more fully and more obediently in You. In Jesus' name. Amen.

Surrender Principle

I am not in control of others or outcomes.

---

1. Barb Roose, *Winning the Worry Battle: Life Lessons from the Book of Joshua* (Nashville: Abingdon Press 2018), 158.

Letting Go of Toxic People

People will be lovers of themselves, lovers of money, boastful, proud, abusive.... Have nothing to do with such people. (2 Timothy 3:2, 5b)

Some people do not want to do what is healthy or helpful for their lives. However, denying their behavior and not enforcing our personal boundaries can create suffering on top of our pain.

Although it's hard to admit, deep down we hope that if we love someone enough, then they will love us enough to stop making our lives so miserable.

While we're called to love people unconditionally as God loves them, we're not called to let people walk all over us or cause us harm. Yet, we don't always know how to balance grace with good boundaries.

In his letter to a young pastor named Timothy, the apostle Paul identified the qualities of certain toxic people. As you read through those qualities, pay particular attention to Paul's final instructions to Timothy:

> *People will be lovers of themselves, lovers of money, boastful, proud, abusive, disobedient to their parents, ungrateful, unholy, [3]without love, unforgiving, slanderous, without self-control, brutal, not lovers of the good, [4]treacherous, rash, conceited, lovers of pleasure rather than lovers of God— [5]having a form of godliness but denying its power. Have nothing to do with such people.*
>
> (2 Timothy 3:2-5)

Unfortunately, toxic people are like magnets. When you get in close proximity to them, the magnetic pull of their attitude or behavior draws you in and makes it hard for you to react or respond in a God-honoring way. Even when you have the best intentions related to a toxic person, their goal is to draw you in and encourage you to behave as badly as they are.

This is why Paul instructed believers to have nothing to do with such people. However, letting go of a toxic person doesn't mean you have to let go of *loving* them. It means not giving your time and presence to people who bring out the worst in you.

While Jesus died to save you from your sin, you have a responsibility to save yourself from the toxic people in your life. You might have to do hard things such as limit your time at family gatherings, opt out of certain text threads, or politely decline coffee or dinner invitations. It's not easy, but it is necessary.

Toxic people are still part of God's creation, but you need to keep them at a distance. First Corinthians 15:33 warns us that "bad company corrupts good character." The Holy Spirit is working within you, so don't undermine the Spirit's work by holding onto a relationship that brings out the worst in you!

What are your next steps? James 1:5 encourages you to pray and ask God for wisdom. Then, seek out trusted voices to develop an action plan and provide accountability (Proverbs 15:22).

- Who are the toxic people in your life who make it difficult for you to focus on your faith?
- Are you a toxic person in need of repentance and possibly help to deal with your struggles?

PRAYER: Dear God, I want my responses and reactions to reflect Your character in my life. However, I am struggling with the toxic relationships in my life because I care about ______________________, but they bring out the worst in me. God, I pray for the wisdom to know how to limit their influence in my life. Amen.

Surrender Principle

I am not in control of others or outcomes.

DAY 21

Letting Go of Enabling

You will keep in perfect peace
those whose minds are steadfast,
because they trust in you.
(Isaiah 26:3)

There's a well-known story about a man who'd been hitch-hiking when he fell down an embankment, but he stopped himself before falling off the edge of a cliff. He called out to a passerby to help him.

The passerby got a rope and tossed down the embankment to the grateful man. He called out to the man, "Grab the rope, and I'll pull you up to safety."

The passerby began pulling the rope. He tugged and grunted for several minutes, but nothing happened.

The passerby called down, “Are you OK? It doesn’t seem like the rope is moving.”

The struggling man replied, “It’s great down here. Do you mind holding on a little longer while I look around?”

Is there someone in your life who has called for help and you’ve tossed them a rope only to have them reject any help? Perhaps you’ve given lifelines of money, time, a shoulder to cry on, but it seems like you’re doing all the work and they aren’t really interested in helping themselves.

Most of us want to help the people who are hurting in our lives, but there are times when helping is actually hurting someone. Perhaps you’ve heard the term *enabling*, which I define as aiding others in staying stuck in their unhealthy behavior.

Only Jesus saves. You can’t. For that you can be grateful! In fact, holding onto someone who doesn’t want help hurts everyone, including you.

Are you enabling because you’re afraid that your loved one might hurt themselves or their future if you don’t intervene? Enabling can look like writing a child’s report when they procrastinate or lying to cover irresponsible behavior. Enabling seems like love, but in reality, you’re just leaving that person on the ledge. The more you try to stop them from going over, the more risk of harm and heartache for everyone involved, including you.

Only Jesus saves. You can't. For that you can be grateful.

At the center of our control-loving enabling is a lot of fear. Our minds spin with endless worst-case scenarios that lead us to believe that their survival depends on us. However, enabling doesn't eliminate pain. It postpones it or makes the situation worse. As long as you prevent a loved one from seeing the reality of their unhealthy actions, they'll never feel the pain that has the potential to lead them to change.

Letting go of enabling means that you hold onto God rather than hold someone back from the consequences of their actions, which prevents them from seeing their need for God. Holding onto God is what gives you peace. When you have God's peace, you stop trying to do for others what they should and must do for themselves. God's peace gives you the strength to not panic when they call and beg you to hold their rope because they don't want to be responsible.

Right now, God has His eye on your loved one, even when they are out of your sight or dangling off the edge of a dangerous cliff. And He is sufficient for them—and for you.

- If you're enabling someone, what are you afraid of?
- What are God's promises for you and your loved one that you need to remember today?

PRAYER: Dear God, I can't keep carrying the weight of _________'s life as well as my own. While I am afraid of what will happen if I step aside, I need to trust that Your salvation and promises are just as true for _____________ as they are for me. Illuminate my control-loving and fixing behaviors so that I can let you be God in ________________'s life. I know You love them and I trust You with their life. In Jesus' name. Amen.

Surrender Principle

When fear tempts me to flee,
fix, or force my way,
I will choose to stop and pray.

DAY 22

When You Thought You Had Let Go

And I am certain that God, who began the good work within you, will continue his work until it is finally finished on the day when Christ Jesus returns.
(Philippians 1:6 NLT)

Have you ever worked so hard to let go of control-loving behaviors only to pick them back up again? Don't beat yourself up! Surrender is a process.

Here's one woman's journey toward surrender, one step at a time:

> For over a decade, I worked feverishly to heal my son from the pain of life's disappointment and his desire to wash it away with alcohol. I

would beg, plead, and lecture him before he would go out. Then, I'd pray that he would not drink.

At the same time, I felt like I was failing as a mom. Was his drinking problem my fault? Was it because his dad had disappeared? Was he suffering because of one of my sins? I wanted so badly to release myself from the pain. I thought trying to control him would make a difference in his behavior.

I would never fully surrender my son because of fear. From the time he was born, I feared that he would die before I did. I can admit now that I made my son into an idol. All of my happiness depended on how he was doing.

A few years ago, he attempted suicide and was hospitalized for a mental health breakdown. After that incident, I was terrified of speaking up because I didn't want to upset him. I was afraid he would attempt suicide again.

Then several years later, he hit rock bottom again. This time, I did too. I finally

> realized that I had to completely let go of him, his life, and his future.
>
> As much as I loved him, my son had to find his own need to change, but as long as I kept intervening, he wouldn't have to. I don't clean up his messes anymore. For me, surrender is a constant process of praying for peace and strength and trust. I've learned that surrender is thanking God in advance for the healing that is to come and accepting whatever form it comes in.

Can you relate to her story in any way? Is there something that you have to surrender over and over again? God won't

Don't focus on your failures, but celebrate your commitment to live like Jesus and walk by faith.

criticize you for taking two steps forward and one step back in your surrender journey.

Don't focus on your failures, but celebrate your commitment to live like Jesus and walk by faith. In fact, today's verse offers some great encouragement for you.

If your heart's desire is to let go and live like Jesus, you don't have to worry that you'll never get it, because God will never give up on you. His Holy Spirit is at work in you and will keep working in you. You keep letting go and living like Jesus and trust that God's victory is coming!

- What are you struggling to surrender these days?
- How does knowing that God won't give up an encouragement to you?

PRAYER: God, I am so grateful that You will never give up on me! Sometimes, it feels like I am taking two steps forward and one step back, yet I am committed to letting go of control of ___________ and choosing to live like Jesus. I trust that You will keep working in my life for as long as it takes for me to learn how to fully surrender to You. Amen.

Surrender Principle

Surrender is my only path to God's peace.

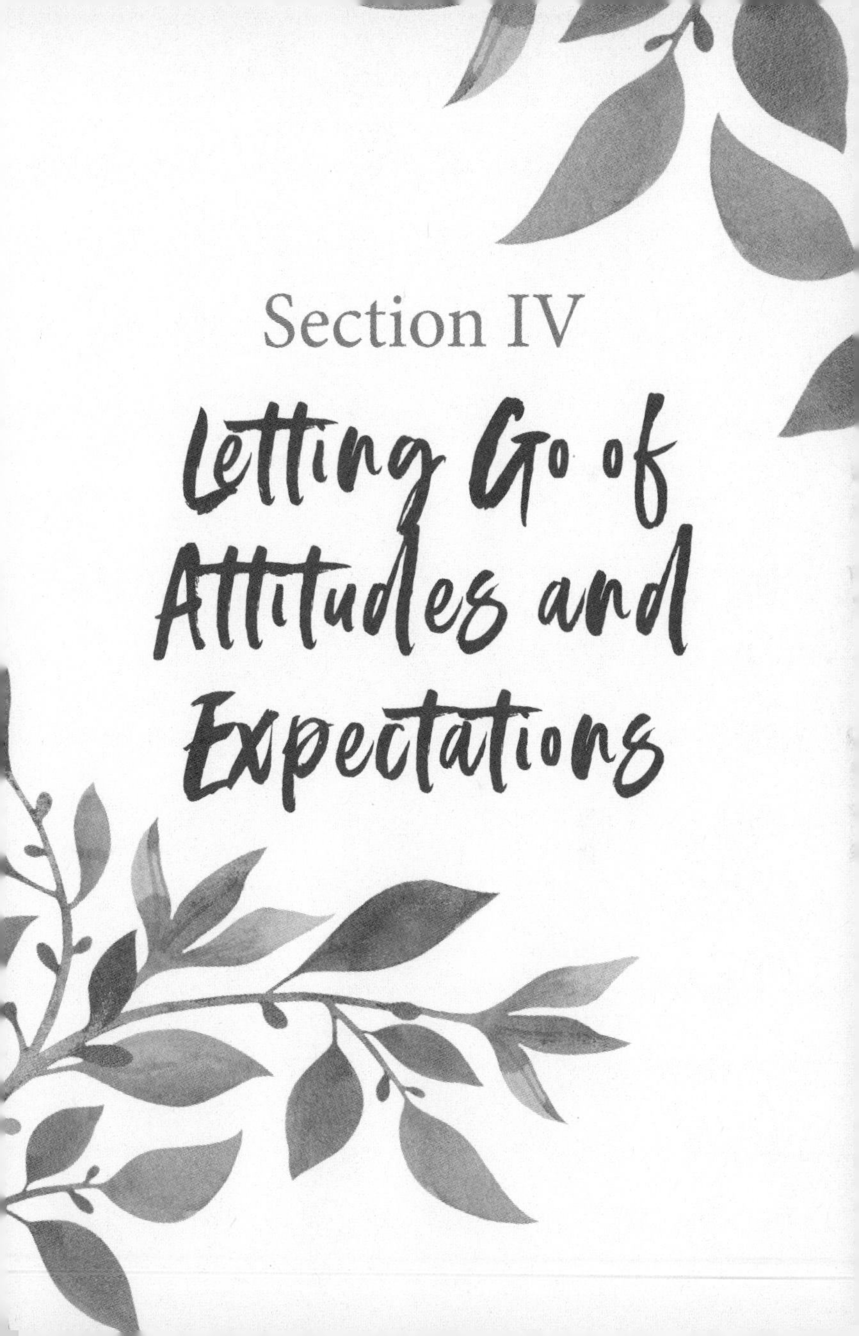

Section IV

Letting Go of Attitudes and Expectations

Letting Go of Entitlement

"'My son,' the father said, 'you are always with me, and everything I have is yours.'"
(Luke 15:31)

When am I finally going to get what I deserve?

Maybe you've muttered those words under your breath while reading an e-mail from your boss. Perhaps you've spit those words out in anger after a visit with your parents or your kids. You feel like you've bent over backwards but you still don't feel appreciated, even though you feel like you've earned it.

Entitlement is the expectation that if we work hard enough, then we'll reap the rewards we want, such as having a certain job, income, home, or well-behaved kids. There's also a spiritual entitlement that most every Christian battles at one time or another.

Spiritual entitlement sounds like, "If I am a good person, then I shouldn't have to suffer." Or, "If I pray enough, then God will give me what I want."

While entitlement isn't a control-loving behavior, it can be related to control-loving behaviors. Entitlement justifies our demand of certain expectations. But letting go of an entitled mindset helps you elevate God's grace over what you think you should get, because you're aware that God has freed you from the consequences of your sin.

In Luke 15, which we explored on day 16, Jesus teaches a group of religious leaders about entitlement in a way that they never saw coming. As Jesus tells the story of the prodigal son coming home, the religious leaders would have squirmed at the idea of grace. Why would the young man be restored to his rightful place after such bad behavior?

Then, Jesus introduces the dutiful older brother who followed all of the rules. The older brother is angry at his father and refuses to come to the welcome home party. "Look! All these years I've been slaving for you and never disobeyed your orders" (Luke 15:29*a*). Then he rails against his father for never giving him what he thought that he deserved.

The tragedy of an entitled attitude is that it erases grace and ignores the abundance of mercy. The older brother, who symbolized the self-righteous religious leaders, clung to his entitled behavior that robbed him of celebrating grace in his brother's life and perhaps recognizing it in his own.

Where does some of that elder-brother attitude show up in your life? When I was growing up as the oldest child, sometimes I had to take on more responsibilities than my siblings. I'd stomp my foot and say, "Dad, that's not fair!" He would reply, "That's because life's not fair."

As a woman who has made her share of mistakes, I'm so glad that life isn't fair! I've been the recipient of God's grace and mercy so many times in my life, and I haven't deserved any of it. But I'll take it!

We don't know if the elder brother ever changed his mind, but Jesus tells us that the father never does. In Luke 15:31, the father tells the elder son that everything that he has belongs to his son. The same goes for you. As God's child through Jesus Christ, you've been promised and given God's very best. You aren't entitled to it because it's already been given to you.

- Where are you struggling with the unfairness of life lately?
- How have you seen God's grace and mercy bless your life even though you don't deserve it?

PRAYER: God, I give thanks for Your grace and mercy in my life. Thank You for all of the blessings that I do not deserve. Thank You that I don't have to earn your love or forgiveness. For the places where life doesn't seem fair, I choose to focus on Your grace rather than the unfairness. Amen.

Surrender Principle

Trusting God's promises will bless me,
but pushing my plans will stress me.

Letting Go of Anger

"In your anger do not sin."
(Ephesians 4:26a)

No one was more surprised than I was when I launched several freshly washed plates from my hands through the kitchen window. In the moments before I hurled those plates through the air, my body felt like a teapot ready to blow. There was so much anger building on the inside that when I finally exploded, the plates in my hands became flying weapons, shattering the large window. Even now, it's embarrassing for me to admit doing such a destructive thing.

Eleanor Roosevelt is often credited with saying, "Anger is one letter short of danger." This is why the Scriptures instruct us to be "slow to get angry" (James 1:19 NLT) and warn us: "In your anger do not sin" (Ephesians 4:26*a*).

Anger is like the frosting on our emotions because it's often covering up something else. Chip Dodd writes, "Anger, therefore, becomes a warning signal, telling us to look inside at what fear, hurt, sadness, or loneliness we're experiencing."[1]

After my anger exploded so dramatically, I sat down with my counselor and spent a long time working through the fear, pain, and hurt around our family addiction crisis. Those big emotions created a thick, creamy layer of anger. But as I worked through the underlying emotions, that layer of anger thinned out and eventually faded away.

Your anger is a serious matter. Paul warned that our anger gives Satan a foothold or a grip to influence us (Ephesians 4:27). Since Satan came to kill and destroy your life (John 10:10), he'd love for you to hold onto your anger against whoever did you wrong. Satan knows that if your anger burns hot enough, he could tempt you toward murder in real life, whether it's killing a person, a relationship, your well-being, or a dream for the future.

If you've been holding onto anger, chances are that there's a lot of pain and hurt you're dealing with. It really is OK for you not to be OK. But, God doesn't want you to stay that way. Therefore, Ephesians 4:26 offers practical wisdom on letting go that you can apply today.

Anger is like the frosting on our emotions because it's often covering up something else.

1. It's OK to be angry, but avoid sin.

Anger isn't wrong. The Scriptures talk of righteous anger; however, sinful or unhealthy anger is motivated by pride, fear, envy, or lack of self-control. As soon as you feel angry, it's time to pray and ask God to help you identify what is happening underneath your anger.

2. Surrender is the path to peace.

One of my surrender principles is, "Surrender is my only path to God's peace." You need to accept the fact that you can't change what's happening in front of you. Once you do that, then you can let go and pray for God's help in walking through it in

His power, peace, and provision. While there may be pain in the moment, surrender keeps you from long-term suffering.

- What's so hard about accepting that we're not always going to get what we want?
- How has holding onto anger been destructive in your life?

PRAYER: God, my anger will not produce the righteous life You want for me. You know that ________________ has been making me angry, but underneath that anger, I feel ________________. God, I need to let go of the desire to get what I want and surrender that situation to You. Amen.

Surrender Principle

Surrender is my only path to God's peace.

---

1. Chip Dodd, *The Voice of the Heart: A Call to Full Living* (Nashville: Sage Hill, 2004) loc 78.

DAY 25

Letting Go of Comfort

Then Jesus was led by the Spirit into the wilderness.
(Matthew 4:1)

Ahhh, the comfort zone.

It's that sweet spot where life is traveling at our desired speed. We feel like we're dancing to our chosen rhythm and our coffee order is always made just right.

But what happens when life shows up and kicks us out of our comfort zone?

> When your steady paycheck goes away…
> When a chronic health diagnosis changes
> your future…
> When your marriage falls apart…

God allows our circumstances to tip us out of our comfort zones so that we can discover that unshakeable peace is found only in Him.

We equate comfort with peace. However, when our comfort is connected to our circumstances, we tend to struggle with finding peace when change swoops into our lives. Therefore, God allows our circumstances to tip us out of our comfort zones so that we can discover that unshakeable peace is found only in Him.

In Matthew 3, Jesus was having a pretty good day. He was standing in the Jordan River being baptized. It was the kind of special spiritual experience that would have looked pretty cool on Instagram. Imagine someone capturing a video of the dove that descended from heaven and God's voice saying "This is my Son, whom I love; with him I am well pleased (Matthew 3:17).

This moment would have felt amazing. It's the kind of moment that we'd want to go on forever.

But everything changes in the very next verse. God's Spirit whisks Jesus into the wilderness and away from the rhythm of life that He knew. The wilderness is the absence of the familiar and comfortable, but it's also an expanse of land completely beyond His control.

There's so much that we can talk about when it comes to Jesus' time in the wilderness. The framework for His experience unfolds in the first seven words of Matthew 4:1: "Then Jesus was led by the Spirit."

While Jesus was alone in the wilderness without comfort, Jesus had a Comforter. God's Spirit went with Jesus into that hard place. God's Holy Spirit is with you in your hard place as well.

Sometimes, you don't know the answer to why your life leaves the comfort zone. Life happens. Often, there's not a neat and easy explanation as to why your way of life has disappeared, dissolved, or been destroyed. If that's what you're going through today, I'm glad you are here.

Jesus knows exactly what you're going through. He spent forty days away from any kind of comfort, with no food and Satan constantly in His face. Yet, Jesus was not alone. God's Spirit was with Him.

And because of what Jesus did later by dying as a perfect sacrifice, He made it possible for God's Spirit to be with you too.

If you're in a wilderness season and you're trying to cling to what you used to know, perhaps you might consider the invitation to let go of your need to be comfortable.

Let go of what makes you feel accepted and acceptable.

Let go of your insistence that your life must flow a certain way.

Let God's Spirit lead you through the unknown wilderness because it is scary. It is uncomfortable, but God's Spirit will guide you and provide for you through His unlimited love and power.

- What do you think you can't live without?
- How can letting go of comfort allow you to experience a greater level of God's peace?

PRAYER: Dear God, this season is hard because so much has changed. I miss the way life used to be! But, I choose to trust that if You are allowing me to be taken out of my comfort zone, then You will take me to a place that is much better for me. In Jesus' name. Amen.

Surrender Principle

I choose to live by faith,
not rush to follow my feelings.

DAY 26

Letting Go of Stuff

"But store up for yourselves treasures in heaven,
where moths and vermin do not destroy,
and where thieves do not break in and steal."
(Matthew 6:20)

Do you remember the great toilet paper chase during the COVID-19 crisis? Around the country, stores reported a toilet paper shortage even though gastrointestinal issues weren't on the list of symptoms.

When we're faced with one situation that we can't control, a natural default is to go overboard on what we can control. One of the SHINE control-loving behaviors is excessive planning or stockpiling. It's motivated by the desire to control any future discomfort or inconvenience by gathering more than what is needed.

When my kids were small, I struggled with the anxious what-ifs. I spent a lot of time buying extras that turned into excess because I didn't like the feeling of powerlessness when I didn't have what I needed. When there was a situation in my life that was out of control, I could go to my stockpile and smile because there was a sweet space where I felt like I was totally in control.

To be clear, gathering extra isn't a sin. In light of bad weather or crisis events like the COVID-19 pandemic, it's good to prepare for emergencies. But for everyday life, it's good to ask yourself if you're gathering extra for an emergency or if you're exposing a control-loving behavior that you need to address. Our stockpiles should never be our source of security.

In Matthew 6:20, Jesus taught that our stockpiles should be made up of treasures in heaven, not overstocking our pantries or linen closets. We store up treasure in heaven when we "use all that we have for the glory of God."[1] So, whether God has given you a lot or a little, it can all be leveraged for an eternal purpose that shines the glory on God, not on ourselves.

Another time, Jesus told the story of a wealthy man who found himself with more than he could manage. The man decided that he would build bigger barns to store up the fruit of his prosperity. The man dreamed of his life after building his barns by saying, "You have plenty of grain laid up for many years. Take life easy; eat, drink and be merry" (Luke 12:19). Then, Jesus calls the man a fool for being rich toward himself but not rich toward God. "Everything was about him, and nothing was about God."[2]

While the man thought he was in control of all that he owned, the man forgot that God was in control over all things. The same goes for you. You can own all of the stuff you want, but when it comes down to it, all your stuff can't save your life. If you're stockpiling because you're afraid of what might happen in the future, you need to recognize that Jesus is your security.

You can lose everything you own in this world, but you can never lose Jesus!

- What do you buy too much of because you're afraid you won't have enough?
- Read Matthew 6:20. What do you need to shift so that you're storing up treasures in heaven rather than stockpiling more here on earth?

PRAYER: God, I want to store up treasures in heaven for Your glory rather than obsess about my stockpiled stuff on a shelf. When I'm shopping, remind me that it's OK to gather extra for emergencies, but for everyday life, I need to put my security in You, not in stockpiling. Amen.

Surrender Principle

Trusting God's promises will bless me, but pushing my plans will stress me.

---

1. Warren W. Wiersbe, *The Wiersbe Bible Commentary: New Testament* (Colorado Springs: David C. Cook, 2007), 25.
2. David Guzik, "Luke 12—Attitudes for Followers of Jesus," Enduring Word, 2018, https://enduringword.com/bible-commentary/luke-12/.

DAY 27

Letting Go of Envy

Rejoice with those who rejoice;
mourn with those who mourn.
(Romans 12:15)

During my divorce, I withdrew from a few of my longtime friends. These precious women had stood by my side throughout years of difficulty and pain. They were my people. Yet, I pulled away.

In that painful season, the green-eyed monster of envy was eating me alive. I wept and admitted to my counselor that I was envious that my friends were still married to their husbands while mine walked away. It hurt to watch them enjoy the empty nest season with their spouses while I started out in that new season of life alone.

Unfortunately, during that tough time, envy seeped into other areas too. On social media, I dreaded seeing pictures of couples celebrating anniversaries or vacations. I struggled through weekend church services because I hated seeing couples leaning on each other during worship or holding hands during the sermon. I'd silently cry, *God, why not me?*

I love Jesus, but oh boy, I had a nasty case of envy.

We never feel good about envying someone, but we still do it. Envy is sneaky because it has two layers. There's an outer layer where we can see what we want and don't have. But there's also an inner layer of belief where the green-eyed monster pops out. It's the place where we're angry or blame God for what He hasn't given to us.

Holding onto envy actually hurts us both spiritually and physically. Listen to the wisdom in Proverbs 14:30: "A heart at peace gives life to the body, / but envy rots the bones." Envy breeds sadness and anger. Those emotions are draining to your soul.

For me, letting go of envy means opening my eyes to what God has already given to me instead of obsessing about what others have.

Look at your own life. Notice everything that God has already provided for you up to this moment. Breathing? Check. Clothes? Check. Not starving? Check. Safe? Check. Whether you're at home or at work, look around at what God has already given to you. God promised to provide everything you need (Philippians 4:19), so the more that you take time to notice, the more you'll recognize God's generosity toward you.

How do you practice surrendering your envy? The key is found in Romans 12:15: "Rejoice with those who rejoice." Rather than feeling envious about your friends' new house, fun vacation, or promotion, celebrate with them! Really celebrate them!

At first, this will be a challenge, but soon you'll discover that celebration builds a bridge to contentment. During my divorce, I decided to acknowledge every wedding anniversary in my social media news feed. It was hard at first, but I kept in mind everything that God had already given to me and I wanted to pay His generosity to me forward by celebrating others. As I celebrated, I felt the life-giving sense of peace because the God who blessed them was still blessing me too.

- When and where does envy show up in your life?
- How can you celebrate with others who are experiencing what you may not have?

PRAYER: God, it's really hard when I see others enjoying what I don't have. Yet, I choose to be intentional about remembering everything that You've given to me. I will rejoice with those who have what I don't have because You've lavishly given me way more than I deserve. Amen.

Surrender Principle

I choose to live by faith,
not rush to follow my feelings.

DAY 28

Letting Go of Rejection

God will never walk away from his people,
never desert his precious people.
(Psalm 94:14 MSG)

When Lara was taken by ambulance to the hospital for a suspected stroke, her husband called her adult daughter to let her know. Lara's daughter said that she'd heard about the stroke but didn't care and wasn't coming to the hospital. A few months later, Lara was at the grocery store and saw her daughter pushing a cart down the same aisle. As soon as her daughter looked up and saw Lara, the daughter wheeled her cart around and went the other direction.

As Lara wept in deep heartache, she wondered, *Where did I go wrong? Why doesn't she want me to be a part of her life?*

Rejection. It is so painful, isn't it?

Did you know that researchers have studied rejection and found that emotional pain is similar to physical pain?[1] This means that the ache you are experiencing is real. Perhaps you're feeling the sharp sting of being abandoned, ghosted, or publicly humiliated. You don't have to deny it or minimize its impact on your heart, even if the rejection happened a long time ago. No matter how or when it happened, rejection hurts.

Do you think Jesus can really understand how badly you're hurting over the love or connection you've lost? The answer is yes! As Isaiah describes the rejection that the Messiah would face, he also writes that He was "a man of suffering, and familiar with pain" (Isaiah 53:3). Pain is often described as physical, but suffering is also emotional. Jesus experienced the same kind of emotional anguish that feels like it is draining the lifeblood from your soul.

Jesus knew that He would be rejected before He ever stepped into our world. Centuries before Jesus' birth, the prophet Isaiah wrote that He would be "despised and rejected by mankind" (Isaiah 53:3). Jesus came to earth knowing that God's chosen people, Jesus' own people, would not only say no to having a relationship with Him but also voice the ultimate rejection when they shouted, "Crucify him!" (Matthew 27:22).

Letting go of rejection is about ruthlessly leaning into God's foundation of love and connection that another person can never take away from you.

There's the temptation to believe that if the person who rejected you came back, then you would feel all better. Yet, the rejection would still have happened and you'd likely live in fear of it happening again.

Letting go of rejection is about ruthlessly leaning into God's foundation of love and connection that another person can never take away from you. That foundation is constructed of two parts: a spiritual pillar and a practical pillar.

Spiritual Pillar

Trust that God will never abandon you, even if you've rejected Him.

God's love for you cannot be lost or earned (Romans 5:8). His love is steadfast, and you can always count on it (Romans 8:38-39).

Practical Pillar
QTIP—Quit Taking It Personally

Other people's actions do not determine your worthiness for love or connection.

- How does holding onto rejection hurt your heart?
- What does Jesus' example teach you about rejection that helps you let go today?

PRAYER: God, I need to ruthlessly lean into Your love for me. I am so grateful that You will never leave me. Fill my heart with the knowledge of Your love and heal the wounds of rejection so I can live full of hope again. In Jesus' name. Amen.

Surrender Principle

I am not in control of others or outcomes.

---

1. Ethan Kross, Marc G. Berman, Walter Mischel, Edward E. Smith, and Tor D. Wager, "Social Rejection Shares Somatosensory Representations with Physical Pain," Proceedings of the National Academy of Sciences of the United States of America, April 12, 2011, www.pnas.org/content/108/15/6270

DAY 29

Letting Go of Perfectionism

Therefore confess your sins to each other and pray for each other so that you may be healed. The prayer of a righteous person is powerful and effective.
(James 5:16)

Just keep it together until after Bible study.

I begged my tears to stay put as I drove down the road toward my women's Bible study group. For many summers, our group met at a friend's house around her pond to study and pray together while our kids laughed and splashed in the water.

On that particular day, I had my very first counseling appointment scheduled right after the Bible study. Everything about me teetered on a razor-thin edge. But, I didn't want anyone to know I needed help.

As far as rest of the world was concerned, I was a good mom who was extra attentive to her kids. No one saw the complex mental gymnastics I did each day to control everything at home, keep it together at work, and most of all, never let anyone see me sweat.

The reality was that I felt like a hot mess in a handbasket. I knew that if I allowed even one crack in the perfect facade I'd created, my entire persona would come crumbling down.

When I arrived at Bible study, I got out of the car and slipped my sunglasses over my reddening eyes. Bless the sun! We opened our Bibles and talked politely about polite things until one friend burst into tears and cried out, "I can't take it anymore."

This was one of the most admired women in our church, who attended every single weekend. There she was spilling the difficult details of her life.

There was something about the eruption of her pain that pushed me over the edge. Before I could stop the tears, they flooded down from behind my sunglasses. I tried to hide them but couldn't.

What happened next changed my life for the better.

On that day, I became real.

The walls of my perfectly crafted facade came tumbling down as I talked about my fears and the shame of being a less than perfect mom. A beautiful flow of love and freedom showed up and settled in our little circle that day, changing me. Forever.

Letting go of perfectionism is all about being real with other believers. No one's life is perfect. We've all got problems. While we might be afraid of how people will react or respond when we're honest and vulnerable, James 5:16 teaches us to be transparent anyway.

When we are real with how we feel, freedom flows into our lives. Trying to hide our sin and our struggles is like tying ourselves up with our own rope. But when we're real, the people around us not only help us find freedom but also walk beside us in faith so that we can keep walking in freedom!

Trying to hide our sin and our struggles is like tying ourselves up with our own rope.

- What are you hiding from others because you want them to see you all shiny and put together?
- Is your desire to be perfect keeping you from experiencing the precious promise of freedom in Christ?

PRAYER: Dear God, I want to be real. I am tired of pretending that I have it all together or that certain problems aren't a part of my life. Give me the courage to talk with the trusted voices in my life and tell them the truth. I want to experience the life-giving hope, peace, and freedom that comes from confessing my sins both to You and to others. In Jesus' name. Amen.

Surrender Principle

Surrender is my only path to God's peace.

DAY 30

Letting Go of Pride

And being found in appearance as a man,
he humbled himself.
(Philippians 2:8a)

Do you ever hear a little whisper inside that says, "I can help them, if they would only listen"?

While we know that we don't have all the answers in the world, we feel like we have a lot of good advice about how others should think or live. Did you know that this well-meaning little whisper has a name? It's called pride.

We don't like to think that our well-meaning advice, suggestions, or even assistance counts as pride. We're just trying to help, right?

Here's the truth about pride: it often lurks under the surface of our best intentions. We want the best for others, but it's pride that whispers that *our* way is what is best for them.

As a Jesus-loving woman, it's hard for me to admit to being prideful. I don't walk around with the attitude that I am better

We want the best for others, but it's pride that whispers that our way is what is best for them.

than others. In my life, fear is often what exposes my pride. I've noticed that when I am afraid for others or trying to avoid a negative outcome, my pride will tell me that I can save everyone and everything from harm.

Can you relate?

In Matthew 4:8-9, Satan takes Jesus to the top of a mountain. He shows Jesus all the kingdoms of the world and he whispers a tempting offer into our Savior's weary and hungry ear: "Listen, this could all be yours. If you bow down and worship me instead of God, then I could put you in control over all of this."

Here's a provocative question: if Satan offered you complete control so that you could protect yourself and others, fix broken relationships, or rescue a loved one and get them back on track, would you be tempted to say yes?

Thankfully, Jesus says no to Satan. More than just saying no, Jesus declares in Matthew 4:10 that, "You must worship the LORD your God / and serve only him" (NLT). Jesus didn't just say that He would worship God alone; he says "you," which could be directed toward the Satan who schemed once more to exalt himself.

Satan tempted Jesus to be prideful and elevate Himself above others. However, the Gospel writer captures Jesus' humble attitude, which is why Jesus said no to temptation.

> *And being found in appearance as a man,*
> *he humbled himself*
> *by becoming obedient to death—*
> *even death on a cross!*
>
> *(Philippians 2:8)*

While Satan presented Jesus with an option to have total control and His way, Jesus rejected the temptation of pride and submitted Himself humbly to God's way.

Letting go of pride is allowing God's power to flow in and through us rather than forcing others to bow to our control. Most times, God's power looks like loving others in a way that allows God's glory to shine through us rather than our own glory of getting what we want.

When we let go of pride's destructive power, we get a chance to see God's power doing "immeasurably more" than we could ever ask or imagine (Ephesians 3:20), both in our lives and the lives of those we love.

- Where can you see evidence of pride in your control-loving behaviors?
- Is there any pride that you need to confess to God today?

PRAYER: God, You are the King of my life. I confess my pride and all the times when I've tried to overpower others because I thought I knew what was best. In Jesus' name. Amen.

Surrender Principle

I am not in control of others or outcomes.

DAY 31

Letting Go of Criticizing Others

Kind words are like honey—
sweet to the soul and healthy for the body.
(Proverbs 16:24 NLT)

A beautiful aroma filled the room as the expensive perfume dripped off Jesus' chin onto the floor. A woman, later revealed as Mary of Bethany, could have sold that perfume for more than a year's wages. Each drop could have equaled a piece of bread. Instead, that perfume was poured out in an act of lavish love toward Jesus.

Not everyone in the room enjoyed the moment. Some criticized Mary, chastising her choices and commenting about what she should have done. Their attitudes were unpleasant and their words were unkind. One translation says, "They scolded her harshly" (Mark 14:5*b* NLT).

Perhaps you know what it feels like when a coworker yells because you didn't do something correctly. Maybe you carry memories from your childhood of a parent who never felt like you did anything right. No one likes to feel the slash of cutting words that reduce us to feeling less than or not good enough.

While it's OK for us to disagree with others about their choices or actions, being critical toward others looks like the following equation to me:

Difference of Opinion
+ Unkind Words
= Critical Behavior

Basically, criticism is the control-loving behavior that says, "I'm right, you're wrong, and I'm going to beat you up with my words for being wrong." When you're critical toward others, everyone loses, no matter how right you may be.

Look closely at the word *criticism*. Notice how many I's are in the word. Like the "I" in *interrupting*, all of the I's in the word *criticism* remind me that when I am critical, I am making someone else's decisions or choices all about me.

Like many other types of control-loving behavior, our criticism wears others down. Letting go of criticism means that we can disagree with others without destroying them with our words. We do this by embracing the wisdom of Proverbs 16:24 and praying for kind words to use when we don't agree with how someone thinks or lives.

I love how Jesus came to Mary's defense in the face of those who criticized her. He said, "Leave her alone. Why criticize her for doing such a good thing to me?" (Mark 14:6 NLT). Jesus pushed back against her critics and praised Mary for her choices.

Your kind words breathe life into the people you're around. Even when you're in conflict with someone, you can speak kindly to them. One year, I chose Proverbs 16:24 as my verse for the year. I turned it into a prayer that I prayed each morning:

> God, give me kind words, a kind heart, and a kind attitude toward others. Amen.

God used that prayer to transform not only my words but also my heart. As I disciplined myself to speak only kind words and eliminate critical ones, my family members flourished. I could still speak truth and address problems, but they knew that my words would never slice their souls.

If you find that your words tend to be more critical than kind, consider making Proverbs 16:24 your prayer for the next seven days.

- Whom do you tend to criticize most often? Why?
- What are some of the unkind words or phrases that you need to eliminate from your vocabulary?

PRAYER: God, please help me use kind words, have a kind heart, and show a kind attitude to everyone I see today, especially those I disagree with. In Jesus' name. Amen.

Surrender Principle

Trusting God's promises will bless me,
but pushing my plans will stress me.

DAY 32

Letting Go of Comparison

For we are God's masterpiece. He has created us anew in Christ Jesus, so we can do the good things he planned for us long ago.
(Ephesians 2:10 NLT)

Who have you been comparing yourself to lately?

Just because you love Jesus doesn't mean you're immune from wondering if some women in your Bible study are more favored by God because they have fewer wrinkles or can eat dessert without gaining weight.

For years, I compared myself to any woman who had beautiful, straight teeth.

I'd see her teeth and my thoughts and feelings would bounce back and forth between longing and guilt. In one moment I would think, *If I had beautiful teeth like that, I would never stop smiling and would feel really beautiful.* In the next moment, guilt would set in and I would beat myself up for comparing myself.

Comparison is a control-loving tool that our culture, including Christians, uses to shame, guilt, or judge women for being not pretty enough, smart enough, spiritual enough, talented enough, or successful enough. Comparison sounds like, *If you want to be worthy, loveable, or acceptable, then you need to try harder.* Comparison is dangerous because when you are stuck in the lie that you are less than, then you act and live like you deserve less than God's best.

Unfortunately, many Christian women feel like talking about our physical appearance isn't a spiritual topic. The reality is that God is the creator of beauty. When we don't know God's perspective on beauty, then our culture will own the conversation. The result is rampant comparison and competition, bringing discouragement and depression to women of all ages and stages in life.

Take a moment and imagine yourself standing in front of a mirror. Imagine God standing next to you, listening to your inner thoughts as you criticize and compare yourself to the women around you. What would He hear you saying? Take a moment to listen closely to what God would say to you. It might sound something like this:

You are my masterpiece. You are treasured and beautiful. I made no one else like you because I specifically wanted you to be in this world.

(Inspired by Genesis 1:31; Psalm 139:13-14; and Ephesians 2:10.)

So, how do you let go of comparing yourself so that you can fully embrace God's beautiful truth? First, you need to know God's truth. One of my favorite tools to help me tap into Jesus' peace is something I call my "God-Morning" technique. Write down five Bible verses about your identity, such as Ephesians 2:9-10 and Psalm 139:13-14. Tape them on your bathroom mirror so that you can look into the mirror and repeat those verses each day until they're seared inside your heart. Those promises will cover your heart in Jesus' peace and protect it as you navigate each day.

When it comes to other women, you can shut down the mental match-up by engaging in the opposite of comparison, which is complimenting. In my *Beautiful Already* Bible study, I explain it like this: "Challenge yourself to stop mentally competing with other women. Choose instead to compliment others, letting them know that you are for them, rather than competing against them. You'll be amazed at the number of women who will be uplifted and encouraged by your words. It's a strategy that will enable you to win too!"[1]

- How often do you look at other women and feel less than?
- If God were standing next to you, what would He whisper to you?

PRAYER: God, it's hard for me to admit that I struggle with comparing myself to other women. It's time for me to let go of the guilt, shame, and lies and embrace Your beautiful truth about me. Thank You that you made me to be a treasured and beautiful masterpiece. In Jesus' name. Amen.

Surrender Principle

I can always let go and give my problems to God.

1. Barbara L. Roose, *Beautiful Already: Reclaiming God's Perspective on Beauty* (Nashville: Abingdon Press, 2016), 34.

DAY 33

Letting Go of Judging Others

"Why do you look at the speck of sawdust in your brother's eye and pay no attention to the plank in your own eye?"
(Matthew 7:3)

I remember an awful day during our family's addiction crisis years ago when I shook the evidence in front of a loved one's face. When an admission of guilt didn't come, I was angry. I finally had proof, and I threatened to expose and embarrass them if they didn't own up to their behavior. In that awful scene, I had a right to be angry about the situation, but I was completely wrong in my attitude and actions.

We judge others when we think the worst of them, assigning motives to their behavior, or we treat them badly because they didn't live up to our personal preferences or values. While God never calls us to give unconditional approval of behavior, judging others prevents us from obeying God's command to love others unconditionally.

Unfortunately, for the control-lover, the feeling of being right is often fuel we use to power up our control-loving behaviors.

In Matthew 7:3, Jesus confronts people who love to point out where others are wrong. Jesus warns them that the little speck of shortcoming that they're judging in others is nothing compared to the giant blinding plank of sin that is wrecking their own relationship with God. "We all have a blind spot... shaped exactly like us."[1] The problem is that either we don't see it or we don't tune into the damage it's causing.

The bottom line of Jesus' illustration is that we've got enough sin and shortcomings in our own lives to keep us busy and out of other people's business. Letting go of judging others means that we stop scrutinizing others' lives and start keeping the focus on ourselves.

How do we break the habit of judging others, especially the people in our lives who are struggling?

1. "Be curious, not judgmental."[2]

Asking questions creates an opportunity for understanding and compassion. When you understand more about where a person comes from and what they've been through, you can begin to see them as God sees them.

2. Respond instead of reacting.

When someone does something you don't agree with, don't voice your gut reaction. Instead, here are some phrases that convey you care without passing judgment:

> You are important to me, so I will be praying.
> Thank you for sharing that with me.
> I trust that you will figure this out.
> I love you and want God's best for you.

3. "Keep your eyes on your own Hula-Hoop."[3]

Twirling a Hula-Hoop takes a lot of concentration. You can't twirl well if you're trying to help someone else twirl. Just as you can't help someone else twirl and keep your hoop up at the same time, you can't fix someone else's life beause you've got enough work trying to navigate your own. Prioritize your own self-examination and prayer. As you humbly acknowledge your shortcomings before God, you'll be less likely to beat others over the head with your personal measuring stick.

- When do you fight to be right? Why is being right so important to you?
- How can you keep your eyes on your own Hula-Hoop today?

PRAYER: Dear God, I don't want to wreck my relationships over trying to be right. Open my eyes to the planks in my eyes that I've been ignoring. Help me break the habit of judging others so I can love people as You do. In Jesus' name. Amen.

Surrender Principle

Trusting God's promises will bless me, but pushing my plans will stress me.

---

1. Junot Díaz (@JunotDiazDaily), "We all have a blind spot . . .," Twitter, November 24, 2012, 6:32 p.m., https://twitter.com/JunotDiazDaily/status/272498015321853953.
2. *Quotes . . . : Vol. 20: Motivational and Inspirational Life Quotes by Walt Whitman* (The Secret Libraries, 2016).
3. Barb Roose, *Surrendered: Letting Go & Living Like Jesus* (Nashville: Abingdon Press, 2020), 103.

Section V

Living Like Jesus

DAY 34

Forgive Like Jesus

"Father, forgive them, for they don't know what they are doing." (Luke 23:34 NLT)

Are you reluctant to read this devotion because just thinking about forgiveness makes your skin crawl? If that's you, I'm glad you're here. Even if you're not ready to forgive, my hope is that, as you read about Jesus' experience with forgiveness, you'll consider whether or not there's a next step that you might apply to your life.

There's a lot of confusion about what forgiveness is and isn't. To be clear, forgiveness doesn't mean you're giving someone a free pass for hurting you. If you need to call the cops to report a crime, don't let anyone stop you! Likewise, forgiveness doesn't mean that you should maintain a relationship with someone who is still engaged in bad behavior or won't acknowledge their bad behavior.

Forgiveness is a form of surrender because you're trusting that God will make right more than what you've been wronged.

So then, what is forgiveness?

> Forgiveness is a form of surrender because you're trusting that God will make right more than what you've been wronged.

As much as we know that we should forgive, the barrier to forgiveness is our pain. Our painful memory screams, "They have to pay for this!" Yet, Jesus shows us how we can forgive, even in the midst of our pain, so that we can begin to experience God's healing and restoration in our lives.

As Jesus hangs on the cross with the nails in His hands and feet, He speaks eleven extraordinary words while in agonizing pain:

> *"Father, forgive them, for they don't know what they are doing."*
>
> (*Luke 23:34 NLT*)

Did you get that? Jesus forgave out of His pain. Jesus didn't wait until after He was resurrected and pain-free. He extended forgiveness as the blood flowed from the crown of thorns atop His head and the spikes that split His skin. Most remarkably, Jesus forgave even though the people weren't even sorry.

Did Jesus' act of forgiveness mean that He gave the people a free pass on what they'd done to Him? Not at all! As one scholar notes, "Certainly both the Jews and the Romans were ignorant of the enormity of their sin, but that could not absolve them."[1] Romans 6:23 explains that the wages of sin is death, but Jesus' death gave us the free gift of salvation.

Jesus forgave because He trusted God's plan for redemption and peace instead of taking out revenge because of His pain. Jesus knew that God's power to redeem the future was greater than the pain that Jesus experienced in the present.

Forgiveness isn't about a feeling. It's about faith in God and a readiness to be healed instead of waiting for the hurt to go away.

If you've been struggling to take a first step toward forgiveness, here is a four-word prayer that is a huge and powerful step of faith: "God, I forgive them."

As you take earnest steps toward forgiveness, God will be healing your heart and mind. Forgiveness releases God's power in your life to make right far more than you've ever been wronged.

- Whom have you been struggling to forgive?
- Imagine what impact forgiveness will have on your heart, mind, and life. What would that look like for you?

PRAYER: God, I want to forgive, but it's so hard for me to forget the pain. Yet, I want to live like Jesus, even in this. So today, I choose to forgive ________________ in faith that You have the power to make right everything that they did wrong to my life. In Jesus' name. Amen.

Surrender Principle

I choose to live by faith, not rush to follow my feelings.

1. Warren W. Wiersbe, *The Wiersbe Bible Commentary: New Testament* (Colorado Springs: David C. Cook, 2007), 221.

DAY 35

Have Peace Like Jesus

"Peace I leave with you; my peace I give you. I do not give to you as the world gives. Do not let your hearts be troubled and do not be afraid."
(John 14:27)

One friend discovered that her husband of more than twenty years was having an extramarital affair. Even as she felt big emotions such as anger, fear, hurt, and grief, my friend ruthlessly dedicated herself to prayer, meditating on Scripture, and listening to worship music.

As we talked in our small group about trusting God in circumstances that we can't control, she said, "I don't understand the way that I am right now. Even though I have no clue about what's going to happen, I have God's peace. It's amazing. Rather than being shattered, Jesus is making me stronger than I've ever been."

How could my precious friend have peace while her world was still falling down around her? In John 14:27, Jesus explains why His gift of peace is a game changer for us, especially when we're feeling afraid and alone during a trial or wilderness season.

Jesus acknowledges that there are two kinds of peace: His peace and the world's peace. Jesus' gift of peace flows from His victory over death on the cross. However, the world's peace lasts only as long as there's money in your bank account, food in your cupboard, or your kids are behaving. Even when we have the world's peace, we're always worried that it can be taken away (and it can).

Praise God that Jesus' gift of peace isn't going anywhere!

Since Jesus is your peace right now, you can stand in uncontrollable circumstances with a calm heart, even if you're crying or having a bad day. That's OK! In Jesus, you still have all that you need. George H. Morrison has defined peace as "the possession of adequate resources."[1]

Jesus *is* everything that you need. He wants you to experience His life-giving, heart-healing peace even as the cancer treatments aren't working, as the layoffs are being announced, while your prodigal is still gone, or even when you're lost and unsure of what to do next. Jesus is still your peace! (Ephesians 2:14).

Here's an important note: just because you're going through a hard time doesn't mean that you've done something wrong or that God doesn't love you. Not at all! Long ago, the psalmist wrote that God is close to the brokenhearted; not only that, the righteous person has many troubles, but God rescues him from them all (Psalm 34:17).

How can you have peace like Jesus today? You can use the "God-Morning" technique from day 32. Read those five verses

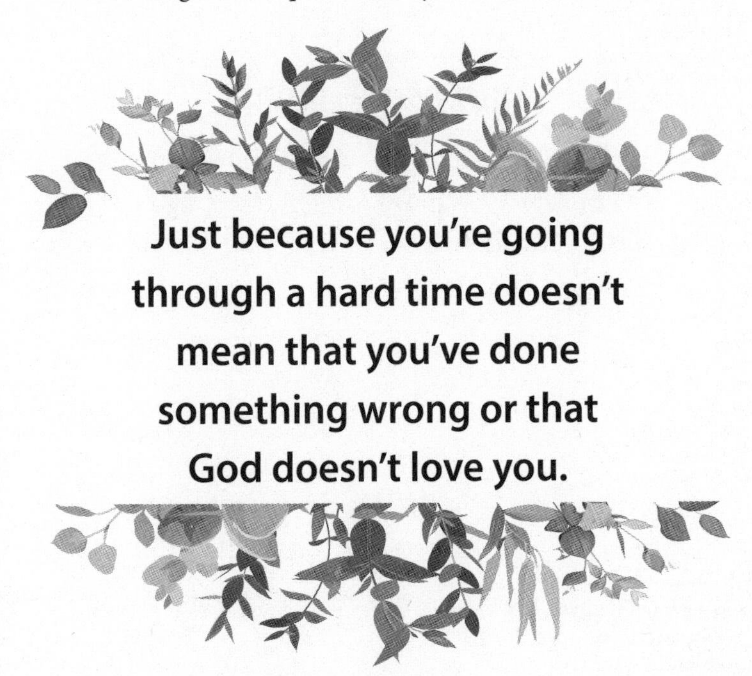

Just because you're going through a hard time doesn't mean that you've done something wrong or that God doesn't love you.

when you wake up and before you start thinking about your day. Those promises will give you Jesus' peace.

- Where do you need peace today?
- What Bible verse about God's peace can you meditate on today?

PRAYER: Thank You, Jesus, that You are my peace! Even in the midst of my problems and my pain, You have given me everything I need so that I can have a calm heart, a focused mind, and open hands. Jesus, I will focus on You today. Amen.

Surrender Principle

Trusting God's promises will bless me,
but pushing my plans will stress me.

1. Warren W. Wiersbe, *The Wiersbe Bible Commentary: New Testament* (Colorado Springs: David C. Cook, 2007), 293.

DAY 36

Obey Like Jesus

In fact, this is love for God: to keep his commands.
(1 John 5:3)

When my kids were small, I taught them this little saying about obedience:

> Obedience is doing what I'm told to do,
> When I'm told to do it,
> with a smile on my face and joy in my heart.

Even as my little girls hated repeating those words, I wanted to help them grow their obedience muscle, and that required practice. My sweet little cherubs didn't understand that obedience would be necessary to protect their well-being, their safety, and their future. All they knew was that even though they hated doing their chores, I loved them; and they trusted (on most occasions) that whatever I asked them to do was for their good.

Though this little saying is not meant to be a theological statement, it does remind me of this biblical truth: God loves you and me, and whatever He asks us to do is for our good. When you say yes to God, it's out of gratitude for God's love shown in His presence, power, and provision in your life. In fact, 1 John 5:3 teaches that obedience is evidence of your love for God.

One Sunday, I felt the Spirit's whisper to visit someone at the hospital. This was a person I'd had a difficult relationship with for more than a decade. Not a cell in my body wanted to say yes to God's prompting, but I drove to the hospital anyway. I complained to God in my heart the entire time riding up the elevator. I followed through on God's prompting that day and patted myself on the back. The next day, I felt God prompting me to go back. It was a struggle, but I did what God asked.

I visited every day for a week. Those hospital visits eventually led to an opportunity for reconciliation. Being obedient wasn't easy, but it was worth it.

In three separate prayers in the garden of Gethsemane, Jesus asks God to release Him from the brutality of the crucifixion and death. "My Father, if it is possible, may this cup be taken from me. Yet not as I will, but as you will" (Matthew 26:39). Another writer captured this moment by saying that Jesus humbled Himself and became obedient to death on a cross (Philippians 2:8). However, Jesus' obedience flowed from His heart, and He followed through in His actions. What Jesus did wasn't easy, but it was worth it for us.

Jesus didn't try to change or control the outcome of His obedience. He did what God called Him to do and left the rest to God. The same goes for us. As Charles Stanley says, "Obey God and leave all the consequences to Him."[1]

God loves you enough to guide you one step at a time. He knows how to bring together all the puzzle pieces that create the big picture. He also knows that you can't do what He can, so He's only assigned you the part you can handle, which is doing what He tells you to do.

- Is there something that you sense God telling you to do OR to stop doing?
- What's one yes that you need to say to God more consistently?

PRAYER: Dear God, today I choose to say yes to what You are calling me to do, whether it's to let go of a control-loving behavior, to forgive, to surrender, or anything else that You call me to do. In Jesus' name. Amen.

Surrender Principle

Surrender is my only path to God's peace.

---

1. Charles F. Stanley, "Life Principle 2: A Life of Obedience," InTouch Ministries, July 2, 2014, www.intouch.org/read/life-principle-2-a-life-of-obedience.

DAY 37

Trust Like Jesus

We do not know what to do, but our eyes are on you.
(2 Chronicles 20:12b)

In the poem "The Road of Life," the writer describes life like riding a tandem bicycle. At first, the writer describes feeling in control of where he is going and the speed at which he is getting there. Then, Jesus suggests that they change places. The writer describes Jesus' approach to being in the lead. In his poem, he expresses the wild adventure and also his reaction to it all.

"It was all I could do to hang on! Even though it looked like madness, He said, 'Pedal!'"[1]

Can you imagine yourself on the back of Life's bicycle and Jesus on the front yelling for you to pedal? While I've got adventure in my bones, I like to be in the front seat determining the direction and speed I want to travel. However, the writer allowed Jesus to be in the front seat, and he kept pedaling because the writer trusted Jesus even though the writer no longer had control.

While faith is getting on the bike, trust happens when you pedal. Even when your life looks completely out of control, Jesus knows exactly where He's taking you. One writer observes, "Trusting God does not mean believing he will do what you want, but rather believing he will do everything he knows is good."[2]

Jesus isn't like the people in your life who quit on you or don't keep their promises. He already proved that He could be trusted in going to the cross on your behalf. Jesus also knows that every journey has dark seasons, but when you stand in eternity and look back on our journey, you'll see that every twist, turn, and tear was worth it.

There were long years when I felt like the road that Jesus was allowing me to travel wasn't fair, and I wanted off that painful path. The journey was too hard and too scary. When I stopped focusing on the twists and turns, I finally got in synch with Christ. Once my pedaling motions were in sync with His, I felt His life-giving power strengthening me.

You might be pedaling through the treacherous paths of a career change, a move, rebellious children, a failing business, or a lifelong mental health issue. Take your focus off the trial and put it on Christ. As King Jehoshaphat prayed long ago in 2 Chronicles 20:12: "We do not know what to do, but our eyes are on you." Jesus knows where He's going with your life. You can trust Him.

Just for today, keep pedaling. Trust Jesus and stop trying to control the journey. You might have to pedal through some hard places, but you're never traveling alone.

- What's the difference between keeping your eyes on Jesus versus life's tough trails?
- How can you keep "pedaling" toward God today?

PRAYER: God, I am grateful that You know the beginning, middle, and end of my story. While I'm in the middle of my journey, I choose to keep my eyes on Jesus rather than the twists and turns. I believe that Your promises are true for my life, and I will keep pedaling toward them today. In Jesus' name. Amen.

Surrender Principle

Trusting God's promises will bless me, but pushing my plans will stress me.

---

1. Tim Hansel, *Holy Sweat* (Dallas: Word, 1987), 52.
2. Ken Sande, *The Peacemaker: A Biblical Guide to Resolving Personal Conflict* (Grand Rapids: Baker, 2011), 72

DAY 38

Have Faith Like Jesus

"If you have faith as small as a mustard seed, you can say to this mulberry tree, 'Be uprooted and planted in the sea,' and it will obey you."
(Luke 17:6)

Have you ever wondered if God is waiting until you have a specific amount of faith before He answers your prayer? As Christians, we like to say things like, "I must have more faith" or "I feel like I've lost my faith." It's like we see faith as a glass. We believe that our cup of faith must be filled to the tippy top to get our prayers answered by God. We believe God won't answer our prayers if our cup of faith is tipped over and there's only one or two drips left clinging to the side of the glass.

Thankfully, Jesus flips our description of real faith around so that we have hope no matter how much faith is in our cup. Real faith isn't something we leverage to get more from God. Rather, real faith reflects our reliance on God and His power to do the impossible in our hearts and lives.

In Luke 17:6, Jesus told the disciples that if their faith was as small as a mustard seed, they could tell a mulberry tree to be uprooted and planted into the sea. This illustration would have sounded nonsensical to the disciples for many reasons. First, mustard seeds were the symbol of all things small and tiny. So how could small faith command a vastly rooted, long-living tree to be plucked out of the ground and somehow, someway planted into the sea? None of that would make sense!

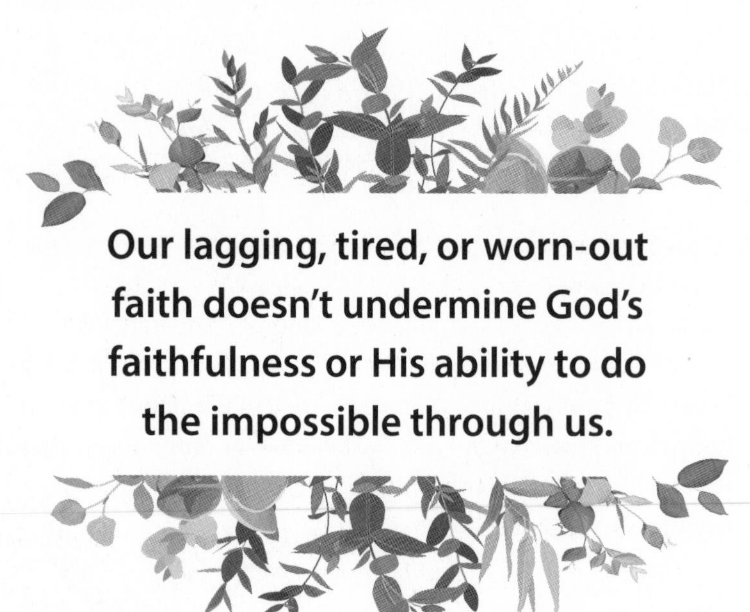

Yet, Jesus used tiny little mustard seeds to teach a hope-giving message on faith: *God's power can do great things through our little faith.*

That's upside-down thinking in our human minds, but God's ways aren't like our ways (Isaiah 55:8), and that's good for us! Our lagging, tired, or worn-out faith doesn't undermine God's faithfulness or His ability to do the impossible through us. But, when we take the faith we have and offer it to God, He strengthens and transforms our hearts, minds, and lives. As God's power works within you, your tiny drops of faith will become a drenching testimony that will overflow and impact the lives of others.

No matter what's in your cup of faith today, offer it to God. Here are some faith statements you can declare over your life and whatever you are facing:

> God, I believe You can get me through this day.
>
> God, I know that You will provide what I need.
>
> God, I trust that You love me.
>
> God, I will give all of my worries and cares to You because You care about me.
>
> God, I know that You are watching over me and everyone and everything that I love.

As you speak these statements over your life, live confidently today that God has heard your declaration and watch out for God's power and provision in your life.

- Where in your life are you struggling with little faith?
- Which one of those faith statements do you need to proclaim with whatever faith you have?

PRAYER: Dear God, thank You for being faithful to me, even when I'm struggling to have faith in You. Today, I proclaim those faith sentences with whatever faith that I do have, and I will choose to trust in You. Amen.

Surrender Principle

I choose to live by faith,
not rush to follow my feelings.

DAY 39

Hope Like Jesus

"I have told you all this so that you may have peace in me. Here on earth you will have many trials and sorrows. But take heart, because I have overcome the world."
(John 16:33 NLT)

We'll always be miserable as long as we believe that we can't be happy until our most painful or persistent problem is solved. But, what if we could still live a happy and joy-filled life even though heartache is an everyday part of our story?

The key to living a joy-filled life is hope. Hope means that just because you can't see how something's going to get done, you know that God can do it! Thomas Merton said, "The real hope, then, is not in something we think we can do, but in God who is making something good out of it in some way we cannot see."[1]

Holding onto hope in the midst of heartache was one of Jesus' final messages before He went to the cross. In John 16:33, He promised that peace and pain would be a part of our human experience in a broken world. But the hope in Jesus' teaching was that peace would prevail because Jesus is our peace and our victory.

Even if we know that Jesus is our peace, how can you live in the tension between peace and pain? I call this tension "holding hope and heartache in both hands."[2] It means that I can accept that good and bad are happening at the same time in my life. Furthermore, I choose to believe that God is good in spite of circumstances that are really bad.

Holding hope and heartache in both hands means that even if you are dangling at the end of your rope emotionally, spiritually, financially, or relationally, God's got you! His divine rope of hope is long enough and strong enough to transcend whatever you're facing today. When you're holding onto God's hope rope, you have peace in knowing that you're held, no matter what happens.

Hope doesn't mean you ignore the real problems you're facing in order to keep up a happy face. Rather, hope blasts the bright light of Christ through your problems and gives glory to God for what He has done, what He is doing, and what He will do in your life.

As a longtime women's Bible study leader, I kick off each group meeting with what I call "celebrations and struggles." As we share our celebrations, we get to hug and congratulate one another. When

Holding hope and heartache in both hands means that even if you are dangling at the end of your rope emotionally, spiritually, financially, or relationally, God's got you!

each woman shares her struggles, we surround her with compassion, love, and prayer. Best of all, as we share our hope and our heartache, we stand together in prayer and invite God to show up in the space between the good and bad in our lives. Together, we experience how God's hope is the rope that helps us live joy-filled lives.

Do you need to grab onto God's rope of hope today? Perhaps, you need to let go of defining a good life as a life without pain or problems and learn to hope like Jesus.

- What are your celebrations and struggles?
- How does Jesus' peace overshadow any difficulties you're facing?

PRAYER: God, I need Your rope of hope because I'm definitely at the end of mine! Today, I surrender my need to have all of my problems and pain go away. Instead, I choose to live like Jesus and trust that I can have peace and hope in the midst of whatever I'm facing today. Amen.

Surrender Principle

When fear tempts me to flee, fix,
or force my way,
I will choose to stop and pray.

---

1. Thomas Merton, *The Hidden Ground of Love: Letters* (New York: Farrar, Straus and Giroux, 2011), 434.
2. Barb Roose, *Surrendered: Letting Go & Living Like Jesus* (Nashville: Abingdon Press, 2020), 164.

DAY 40

Pray Like Jesus

We are human, but we don't wage war as humans do.
We use God's mighty weapons, not worldly weapons.
(2 Corinthians 10:3-4a NLT)

Perhaps you know what it's like to experience questions or confusion around prayer. I don't know how long you've been praying for, over, or against whatever is happening in your life, but if you're like me, prayer can feel complicated. It's hard to pray when prayer feels hard.

While there are lots of definitions of prayer, the simplest definition is that prayer is connecting with God. It includes talking, listening, silence, and even singing. Prayer isn't a prescription that we ask God to fill with a yes to whatever we want. Rather, my friend, the late Jennifer Dean writes that the purpose of prayer is actually "to release the power of God to accomplish the purpose of God."[1]

Prayer is power.

Prayer is power. James 5:16 reminds us that the prayers of the righteous are powerful and effective. Prayer is what moves mountains and changes hearts.

When you pray and desire to accomplish God's purposes, He will empower you in ways that are beyond what you could ever do on your own. One of the principles of Alcoholics Anonymous is that "When I can't see any way out and I doubt that even a Higher Power can help me, that's when I most need to pray. When I do, my actions demonstrate my willingness to be helped."[2]

For many years, I lived with a "to-do list first, pray later" attitude. In my eyes, prayer was like having coffee with God. Since I had problems to fix, I felt like prayer had to wait until I was done.

The reality is that when I pray first, God focuses my heart and mind so that I'm able to *do* things better instead of trying to *make* things better. When I pray first, I've discovered that I actually need to do less because I'm not trying to do "all the things."

Learning to pray like Jesus will be your lifeline when your life seems like it's falling apart. That holy lifeline made it possible for me to keep writing studies, traveling, and speaking even as the pain in my soul cried out to God each day. None of this could have happened without praying first!

What would it look like for you to pray like Jesus—to be intentional about connecting with God throughout the day? God wants to unleash His power in your life, so how will you connect to that lifeline?

If prayer hasn't been a part of your life, here's a simple acronym to get you started. Or, if you need to reconnect that lifeline, this simple tool will give you the jump-start that you need:

> **P**raise God for who He is
> (His character and attributes)
>
> **R**elease expectations
> (your own agenda)
>
> **A**cknowledge blessings
> (what you are grateful for)
>
> **Y**es to God's whisper
> in your life (say yes to
> God's invitations)

- Does prayer feel like a nice coffee chat with God or a power-packed session?
- What needs to happen for prayer to become an everyday, intentional part of your life?

PRAYER: God, it's so hard to pray sometimes, especially when I am afraid my prayer won't be answered the way I want. However, I need to let go of what I want so that I can receive Your power to help me endure and overcome what I'm facing. Amen.

Surrender Principle

I can always let go
and give my problems to God.

---

1. Jennifer Kennedy Dean, *Live a Praying Life: Open Your Life to God's Power and Provision* (Birmingham: New Hope, 2011), 30.
2. Al-Anon Family Groups, *Courage to Change: One Day at a Time in Al-Anon* (Virginia Beach: Al Anon Family Group Headquarters, 1992), 48.

EPILOGUE

The Beauty of the Surrendered Life

"If you try to hang on to your life, you will lose it.
But if you give up your life for my sake, you will save it."
(Matthew 16:25 NLT)

No one ever thinks that the words *broken* and *beautiful* should go together. Broken often means useless or unwanted, while beautiful is usually paired with words such as *flawless* and *perfect*. Yet, our human experience is a mix of broken and beautiful, because that's the world we live in.

At one point in my surrender journey, I asked God to give me a picture of what my healed heart and life could be like one day. There were some painful days when I could almost hear my heart breaking. I needed a vision or a symbol of what my heart could look like rather than a pile of sharp, bleeding shards stuck in my chest.

One day, God showed me a wonderful picture that inspired me to believe my broken heart and life would be beautiful again. It was a picture of a piece of repaired pottery called *kintsukuroi* (kint-su-ku-roi). This word represents a form of Japanese art constructed from broken pottery that has been reassembled and fused together with gold or silver instead of resin or glue. *Kintsukuroi* honors the notion that something that's broken doesn't have to lose value or usefulness. In fact, *kintsukuroi* demonstrates that brokenness can be transformed into something more beautiful and valuable.[1]

After all that's happened in my life, I smile when I picture my heart as a work of God's *kintsukuroi*. It's a symbol of the beautifully surrendered life. While the broken pieces of the pottery reflect our human experience, God picks up the broken pieces of our hearts, reassembles what might feel hopelessly broken, and restores His masterpiece, full of beauty, promise, and purpose.

Long ago, Jesus taught that when we try to hold onto our lives, we'll lose them. To me, that's like holding onto the broken pieces and refusing to give them to God because I want to try to put my life back together on my own. Yet, surrender is giving God the pieces because He knows what to do with them.

God doesn't tell us to glue ourselves back together with our own sweat and effort. Instead, God is the precious gold in *kintsukuroi* because He holds us together with Himself. It's God's power and presence that make you more beautiful in your brokenness.

The beauty of the healed heart and surrendered life is that, when you let go, God does the healing work that you can't do for yourself. Not only that, but as God restores, the new you becomes more beautiful, valuable, and capable because, as God touches the broken pieces, His powerful fingerprint indelibly changes every fragment of you.

Now that you're at the end of your forty-day devotional journey, reflect on how you have seen God bringing beauty from the broken pieces of your life as you have been learning to surrender. Consider how you are now walking closer with God. Thank Him for this healing and for holding you together with His power. My prayer is that you will continue to surrender more and more and experience the fullness of God's healing power in your life.

PRAYER: God, thank You for walking with me through this experience. I praise You for the changes I have seen in my life! I pray that in the days ahead, I will continue to let go and live like Jesus in everything I say and do.

When I'm tempted to keep score, I pray that You remind me to give grace.

When I'm tempted to helicopter or micromanage, I pray that You remind me to trust.

When I'm tempted to interrupt others or not to respect their boundaries, I pray that You remind me to be humble.

When I'm tempted to nag or offer unsolicited advice, I pray that You remind me to be wise and loving with my words.

When I'm tempted to plan excessively, I pray that You remind me to trust in Your provision and not to worry about my future.

Most of all, God, I pray that I will grab onto and never let go of your enduring, faithful promises for my life and the lives of those I love. Amen.

---

1. Tiffany Ayuda, "How the Japanese Art of Kintsugi Can Help You Deal with Stressful Situations," *NBC News*, April 25, 2018, www.nbcnews.com/better/health/how-japanese-art-technique-kintsugi-can-help-you-be-more-ncna866471.